LEADERS OF SOCIALISM

Leaders of Socialism
Past and Present

By

G. R. S. TAYLOR

HX23
.T24

ESSAY INDEX

Essay Index Reprint Series

BOOKS FOR LIBRARIES PRESS

FREEPORT, NEW YORK

First published 1910
Reprinted 1968

LIBRARY OF CONGRESS CATALOG CARD NUMBER:

68-24857

PRINTED IN THE UNITED STATES OF AMERICA

CONTENTS

LEADERS OF SOCIALISM
PAST AND PRESENT

I

ON LEADERS AND LEADERSHIP

IT is not very scientific to take notice of such unimportant things as political leaders and their ideas of leadership. They may be brilliantly attractive, glowingly eloquent, heroically audacious, or inexplicably clever ; they may have thousands or hundreds of thousands of followers ; they may appear of gigantic proportions in the pages of the popular historians. But when all is said that can be said for them, it does not amount to much, when they are drawn in due perspective against the background of the universal stage. The journalist, the novelist, the dramatist, the school child, may all have their ardent views of the powers and possibilities of the great man. The level-headed scientist can only see him as a mere speck on the horizon, or, if you prefer it another way, a bobbing cork in the river of history, floating with the stream, not guiding it. He is the sport of his circumstances, ordered

here and there by world-impulses which he did
not create, which he cannot disregard. But this
miserable slave of destiny has his uses. Although
he does not lead anybody, yet he is quite a convenient indicator, just to show which way the water
is flowing. He is an intelligible summary of a vast
movement which would go on without him, of course,
but would not be easily understood if it were not
compressed into the narrow limits of his petty
individuality. Such is the use we propose to make
of the great man in the following pages ; a convenient summary of the various developments of
the Socialist movement. No single one of these
leaders expresses it with any completeness (perhaps Jean Jaurès does that more than any of the
others), but together they give us a very good
idea of the direction in which they are all being
carried.

That is the rather ignominious scientific valuation
of the great man. He has another side, however.
He is a human being, even though a slave ; he is
entitled to his own little say, for what it is worth.
Even Karl Marx does not get a fair hearing, if he
appears only in the general history of Socialism.
If any one could wave his arms above the current
to the onlookers on the bank, one would suspect
Mr. Bernard Shaw capable of doing it : yet, just
consider the immanent danger there is that he will
be put down by accident as " leader of the Fabian
Society " or by some such ridiculously misleading
description ; when, as a matter of fact, he spends his
life inventing (and believing) revolutionary thoughts

which would scare the peaceful ladies and gentlemen of the Fabian Society beyond repair, if they only understood what he meant. Fancy connecting the creator of Andrew Undershaft, gunpowder maker, with a society whose most valiant ideal is to creep about Downing Street and Spring Gardens in rubber-soled boots, lest any one should get to hear of Socialism ; a Society whose perpetual nightmare is that the world may know that it has designs of any kind whatsoever. Mr. Shaw does not lead the Fabian Society—he is, on the contrary, perpetually giving it away ; it is one of his jokes which has not yet dawned on the members.

So, from motives of ordinary fair play, the individual must be allowed to stand by himself, quite apart from his clubs and associations and parties. In the narrow limits of these pages there is no space to look at each subject from all his sides, and it is the mark of the great man to have many sides. We have endeavoured to pick out the particular characteristic which was, or is, the peculiar mark of each one's leadership ; each one's contribution to the evolution of Socialist thought. Beyond their common acceptance of the main outline of Socialism, each one, it is suggested (and it will be the endeavour in these pages to prove the truth of the suggestion), advanced one further step ; or, rather, expressed clearly a new step which the movement had taken in its progress onwards. Thus, Lassalle and Keir Hardie express the need for political independence, while Jean Jaurès demonstrates the need for a further advance from this independent position until the Socialist Party becomes interlocked with every subject of national or international life.   Saint-Simon and Sidney Webb, in their very different ways, have insisted on the urgent need for precise scientific assistance and expert officials as the foundation of all government.   Karl Marx expresses the great fact that Socialism is based on the dicta of Science ; and William Morris has shown that it is the inevitable basis of sound Art. And so on.   No one of all these men has held the whole truth ; but the sum of all their leadership has brought us to the Socialism of to-day.   As we have already said, Jean Jaurès more nearly expressed the whole than any one else : for he is the exponent of scientific thinking and of political action.   He appreciates the need for the expert, and he feels the full force of the untrained democratic voice, and realizes its value.   In politics he is always asserting the independence of Socialism ; but, with infinite skill, he is continually blending it with every phase of affairs.   He always keeps open the door for each new group to join the Socialist Party as the time becomes ripe ; he keeps in close touch with Trade Unionism, and skilfully expounds what is good in the General Strike, yet never advises it.   He is a brilliant fighter and yet the most cautious of generals.   He is, in short, the biggest cork in the Socialist stream.

To avoid all possible misunderstanding, perhaps it is well to point out what all these men have in common, since it will be only their peculiar qualities which will be discussed under their individual names.

The common bond which connects them all is the belief in Socialism. It is, unfortunately, by no means unnecessary to state that fact; for the essential core of Socialism is continually being overlooked, both by our opponents and also by the more careless-thinking of our friends. The main theory of Socialism is that the private ownership of the instruments of production, distribution, and exchange is the radical evil of present social structure; and that there will be no radical improvement until the ownership by private individuals is supplanted by the united ownership of the whole community or a sufficiently large part thereof. Further, this public ownership must be extended to all these instruments, for to nationalize the factories without nationalizing the land, and vice versa, would leave a loophole which would spoil the whole scheme by giving the capitalist a way of escape. That being the essence of Socialism, it follows that it is the basis of all the various phases of leadership we shall consider hereafter. The scientist Marx and the craftsman Morris, the Social Democratic Hyndman and the Fabian Webb, the Utopian Saint-Simon and the political Jaurès, are all in accord where they preach that collective ownership is the only root-remedy and all else is mere tinkering which leaves the cause of evil untouched. But the chief reason for insisting on this common belief is that it is so important to mark off these leaders of reform from all others who claim that name. Holding, as we must, if we are Socialists, that there is one way, and one way only, of reforming society, by abolishing private monopoly of the instruments of wealth ; it follows that all who do not agree with us on this point are not real reformers at all, in our opinion. If a man is not a Socialist, he is fundamentally on the wrong lines and his schemes are mere sentimental illusions. Henry George with his all-embracing land-tax, and the sweet old lady whose aching soul finds relief in sympathetic charities, in our view are going hand-in-hand on a futile mission which must utterly fail. The most tender-hearted of Liberals and the most callous of Tories are alike in opposing the only remedy which is the slightest good. We are not fighting for sympathy or vague sentiments, we are fighting for Socialism.

Such being the common bond between all the following leaders, it is worth remembering how slight, in the main, are their individual differences ; and when they differ, it is usually because they were surrounded by different circumstances ; and, being great leaders, they modified their actions to suit the position. Fourier stood outside politics because the time was not ripe ; Keir Hardie plunges in because an electorate is waiting to be led. It is not even very wise to retain the usual distinction between the Utopian Socialists before Marx and the Scientific Socialists who followed him. It is, of course, possible to insist on the fact that Saint-Simon and Fourier, with their separate colonies and cults, had failed to grasp that it was the whole social structure as it stood before them which must be moulded into their scheme, that the whole society must evolve, that it was useless for a section of it to revolt. They were certainly Utopians in that they based their plans on the action of a minority, whereas the scientific leader accepts the unpleasant fact that he has to deal with the majority. They were likewise Utopians because they depended on voluntary action, and did not understand that only the State, by political means and by legislation, can deal with such a comprehensive problem. They were Utopian when they failed to see the necessity of founding their own party in the political field. But, after all, if Saint-Simon was a dreamer when he hoped to get anything by a sentimental appeal to the good sense or compassion of King Louis, then the Fabian Society is sentimental when it appeals to the Liberals or the Tories, instead of facing the problem of supporting a Socialist Party to do its own business. On the other hand, if one is only thinking of the Utopians' conception of the ultimate social structure—of Fourier's phalange or of Saint-Simon's college of experts—then, as a matter of fact, they are both as likely to be right as any of the " dreamers " of to-day. Mr. Wells and Saint-Simon have both thought out Utopias ; they are only " dreamers " in the sense that such is a popular description of any man who is wide awake an odd hundred years or so before his fellows.

There are many omissions from the following list of leaders which may be criticized. It may be asked where are Liebkneckt, Bebel, Rodbertus, Engels, Vandevelde, Ferri, Guesde ? In the case of a book for English readers, it may be reasonably demanded why the names of two men are omitted, when they are perhaps as prominent in the public mind as any other Socialists at the present moment; I mean Messrs. H. G. Wells and Ramsay Macdonald. The answer to this criticism is that an attempt has been made to select the men who led the way in each advance in Socialist development. Bebel, for example, is merely applying the doctrines of Marx and the policy of Lassalle to the present situation; in so far as he is modifying the strict doctrine of the Socialist creed in order to support and obtain temporary reforms (for example, an eight-hour act), then that compromise is better illustrated by the work of Hardie and Jaurès. Perhaps Mr. Ramsay Macdonald had a real right to inclusion; for he stands as the chief representative of the new policy of combining the Socialists and the Trade Unions into the political alliance of the Labour Party. But that policy is of such recent growth, and Mr. Macdonald has the advantage of being such a youthful leader, that it would be scarcely fair to judge either him or it beside the maturer movements : it is in the experimental stage. As for Mr. H. G. Wells—he is the Fabian Society out for a holiday, and writing the breeziest of delightful prose; he is what Mr. Sidney Webb would be if he read nothing but poetry for a year and took moonlight walks. They both have views on experts and areas of government; and Socialism is a very sanely scientific creed to both of them. Unfortunately Mr. Wells is just as Utopian and unscientific as Mr. Webb when he gets on the subject of politics. " He has no hesitation in saying that he does not believe a Socialist Party existing by itself is either possible or desirable at the present time. He is more and more resolved not to have anything to do with the development of such a party." This is not because he is fearful of the safety of the Labour Party, for he, apparently, does not hope much from that party either. He meditates on the good that may be got from Liberals and Conservatives. " He regards . . . the almost fanatical anti-Liberalism of some members of the Independent Labour Party as mischievous stupidity." That is Mr. Wells' own account of his politics. He is now the only real believer in the " old gang " policy of the Fabian Society ; he is prepared to sacrifice political activity to the delicate diplomatic needs of permeation. But he converts to Socialism those whom no one else can reach ; and since the whole Socialist movement has repudiated his politics (as it did in the case of his letter to the electors of Manchester, beseeching them to vote for the glories of Liberal reform instead of the visions of Socialism—and that from the creator of Utopias !) he is worth a few lapses into early Victorian political tactics.

It is now fairly clear that the theoretical basis of Socialism is a comparatively fixed quantity ; and there is little dispute thereon. For practical purposes, we can find all the theory we need in the pages of Karl Marx and Sidney Webb. But an equally important matter remains to be discussed.

We know what Socialism is ; the question is : How can we most quickly bring it to pass ? It is a question about which there is practically no dispute on the Continent ; where every great nation has its Socialist Party in Parliament, as a declaration that Socialism can only come by the parliamentary action of an independent political body. In Great Britain the case is by no means beyond the stage of argument ; we have the astonishing spectacle, for example, of Mr. H. G. Wells pleading for the hope in constructive Liberalism and Toryism. Such a thing could scarcely happen in France or Germany, where they long ago settled that they must have their own party of Socialists. England is waiting for its Jean Jaurès who will gather together into one unified parliamentary party all the elements of Socialist attack.

We are waiting in this country for a great leader who will overthrow this popular delusion that Socialism is social reform, that Englishmen are gentle evolutionaries. When a social reformer in England is afraid of his own demands, when he wonders whether he is not getting in the firing line, with danger of a bullet, then he discreetly retires, with the comforting reflection that, after all, it is foolish to try to push the English people into great revolutions, for it is the natural law of their race to go forward very slowly : slow but sure, is the motto of reform in these islands, and it is useless to kick against the pricks. There is more than a doubt whether this soothing theory is based on historical fact or on the nervous imaginations of

timid leaders.   It is all very well for the permeating
Fabians to say that their peculiar creeping method
alone suits the genius of the British people ; they,
at least, overlook such pertinent facts as the quick
change from a despotic monarchy to Oliver Crom-
well, with the illuminating spectacle of a headless
king to drive home the moral of the incident.
Another forty years saw the hurried departure of
Scottish James because his people had taken up
arms on riotous behalf of Dutch William.   And
there have been Wat Tylers and Chartists and other
popular demonstrators who do not, strictly speaking,
come under the head of peaceful evolution.   In
short, it is doubtful whether this " peaceful Englishman " is not as mythical a being as the Englishman
who is a " born sailor."   The day for physical
rebellion is perhaps past ; the day of political revolt
has at last come.   And the symbol and practice of
revolt must take the shape of a Socialist Party that
will challenge all other species of reform.

[Perhaps the most convenient books for those who desire to
get a general view of the Socialist movement are : *Contemporary
Socialism*, by John Rae, M.A., LL.D., and *History of Socialism*,
by Thomas Kirkup.   Both these books are written from the
standpoint of independent criticism.   *Modern Socialism*, a most
valuable book, is a collection of Socialist literature from the
works and speeches of the great leaders, and the programmes of
the chief parties on the Continent and at home ; edited, with
an illuminating introduction, by R. C. K. Ensor.   The annual
edition of the *Reformers' Year Book* is the best summary of the
current affairs of the movement.

II

ROBERT OWEN

1771–1858

Born 1771. At ten assistant in draper's shop. At nineteen manager of cotton-mill, where he introduced improved processes. 1800, moved to New Lanark Mills as partner and manager over 2000 workers there. In 1813, in co-operation with Jeremy Bentham and others, turned the business into trust for philanthropic purposes after paying five per cent on capital. 1817, proposed co-operative colonies as solution of unemployed problem. 1825, founded New Harmony communal colony in United States. 1828, retired from New Lanark and became propagandist of Socialism in form of co-operative industry. Died 1858. Chief books: *New View of Society, New Moral World, Autobiography, Revolution in Mind and Practice of the Human Race.*

MACAULAY has put on record that once, at a fancy ball, he met a man who was engaged, with much enthusiasm, in converting one partner to the principles of co-operation, and another to the doctrine that moral responsibility has no legitimate place in an intelligent code of philosophy. The man was Robert Owen, who lived for eighty odd years teaching the same two essential ideas which filled in the intervals at the ball. The ultimate result of his propaganda was the foundation, in 1834, of the " British and Foreign Consolidated Association of Industry, Humanity, and Knowledge," to aid in the creation of a " New Moral World." The scope of this programme was sufficiently wide to win for Owen the posthumous title of Utopian ; and if that means a man who does not fit into the current rules of society, then he deserved the name. He had been a rebellious person from childhood ; exceedingly sceptical about the worth of accepted truths. The loan of some religious books by a Methodist lady had the unlooked-for result of convincing him, at the age of ten, that there was "something fundamentally wrong in all religions." And when, at nineteen, he found himself, after a rapid rise on his own merits (and the necessary luck), manager over five hundred workmen in a factory, he soon became certain that there was something radically wrong in the affairs of earth as well as in the more remote affairs of heaven. It is the proposal of a revolution in society, which he recommended as the remedy for the evils which surrounded him as a manufacturer and a self-respecting citizen, that entitles him to be placed as the first leader of a conscious Socialist party. It is now half a century since ·Owen died, and it is possible to judge what was permanently valuable in his teaching, and what was accidental and merely the outcome of passing circumstances.

Be it at once understood that Owen during most of his career as an active manufacturer was not a Socialist within the strict meaning of the term ; he was merely a Tory democrat. As a captain of industry (and it must not be forgotten that he was

one of the commercial successes of the Industrial
Revolution) he quickly saw that the iron machine
was but a small part of the manufacturer's equip-
ment ; the human tool was at least as important.
He found this human tool in a state of almost
indescribable rust and wreckage, the result of the
wild anarchy in the age of unrestricted trade competition during the early capitalist period. As a
practical man of business as well as a humanitarian,
he saw that it was ridiculous to expect good work
from the miserable beings who formed the working-
class population. So he set himself to improve
the condition of his work-people ; and his system
was put into practice—so far as he was allowed to
act without hindrance by his short-sighted partners
—at the historical New Lanark Mills, of which
he was a part-proprietor, between 1800 and 1829.
During those years Owen gradually evolved from a
successful manufacturer to a Socialist agitator.

At the very beginning he had grasped one truth
which is at the base of the Socialist position : he
saw that man is essentially a healthy animal in
body and mind, and that what is necessary for his
proper development is a fitting environment. In
other words, man will develop aright, if he is
surrounded by material and immaterial circumstances which form the suitable soil for his roots.
" Any character, from the best to the worst, from
the most ignorant to the most enlightened, may be
given to any community in the world at large by the
application of proper means, which means are, to a
great extent, at the command and under the control

of those who have influence in the affairs of men."
Man, in fact, is the sport of his surroundings.
That was what Owen meant when he tried to convince the lady at the ball that moral responsibility
does not exist ; man is not what he, individually,
tries to be ; he is what his circumstances make him.
It was with this belief that he insisted on careful
attention to the education of the children who
lived within the New Lanark community ; and the
restriction of their labour until a more reasonable
age than the period allowed in other factories.
It was this conviction which made Owen fight so
hard for the factory acts, until he became hopeless of
getting anything worth having from Parliament.
Owen's theory is still the answer to the argument
of our opponents that we are bringing about the
deterioration of the race by giving the people ample
education and ample food.   We answer, with Owen,
that these good things are essential, if we look for
good citizens ;   without the proper environment the
resulting products must be bad.   Owen laid down
the principle that a human being is fundamentally
good.   This optimism is a part of the Socialist
creed, when it asserts that the provision of food,
clothing, sanitary homes, and education, even if all
entirely free of charge to the individual recipient,
must inevitably go towards the healthy development of the being who receives them.   We have a
firm conviction of the natural healthiness of the
human species ; the only things which can harm it
are bad things, and neither food, clothing, a healthy
house, or education is a bad thing : on the con-

trary, they are all essentially good. Owen taught optimism ; the man who dreads pauperization is a pessimist, he thinks that mankind is naturally vicious.

But, so far, Owen was not a Socialist ; for he had not seen that the real evil lay in the fact that the instruments of production and distribution were a monopoly in the hands of a small fraction of the community. In the beginning, the New Lanark Mills were the property of Owen and his partners ; and, however wisely and humanely they might treat their workmen, there was no economic difference between their mill and that of the most abandoned sweaters in the country. However, Owen was evolving rapidly. In 1814 he, with Jeremy Bentham, William Allen, and one or two others, bought out the rest for £114,000, agreeing that after five per cent had been paid on this capital, the remaining profits should be spent on the education and improvement of the workers ; a substantial prospect, seeing that the last four years had shown a net profit of £160,000. Although this was still Tory democracy, the masters had voluntarily made themselves trustees for their men. Then, in 1817, the disorganization of industry which followed the sudden end of the great European wars at the battle of Waterloo, set Owen in search of a remedy for unemployment ; and he propounded his scheme of "villages of unity and co-operation," in which the unemployed were to be collected together into self-supporting communities, where they would co-operate for their mutual support from the produce

of their various labours. In practice the scheme
was, undoubtedly, then unworkable, as it would
probably be to-day ; but, theoretically, it was based
on the principle that the "villages" would get
rid of the capitalist, and produce solely for their
collective good. Here Owen had discovered the
clue to the system which became the final form of
his teaching, and entitled him to be placed as the
first leader of Socialism. Gradually he withdrew
from the New Lanark Mills, where the masters
were endeavouring to rule for the benefit of the
men ; and he went forth to preach the pure Socialist
creed that there was no room in the world for
masters, for the people would never come to their
rights until they owned their own factories and
farms ; not in individual ownership, but as collective
property, shared for the collective good.

Owen had now grasped the scientific basis of
Socialism, that the instruments of production and
distribution must be held in common ownership,
although he was probably only partly conscious of
the sociological laws which rendered that basis
necessary. It is when he passed on to suggest
the method by which this collective ownership
could be formed that he ceased to be scientific
and became a Utopian. Briefly stated, he recommended that the Trade Unions should turn
themselves into productive societies, owning their
own factories ; or that colonies of workers should
be formed on the co-operative principle. Now,
there are two essential fallacies in Owen's proposed
methods of getting to the Socialist State. First,

he thought that it would be possible for a Socialist
community to exist as a self-contained unit in a
non-Socialist country. That is the inherent vice of
Utopians ; to disregard the stubborn fact that
society is an organic unity, and that a healthy part
cannot exist in a diseased whole. Owen's colonies
or trade-union associations would be swamped in the
general world of business conducted in the ordinary
way of individualist competition ; and, further, even
when they formed a majority they would be com-
peting against each other. Secondly, Owen thought
that Socialism could be brought to pass by the
development of Trade Unionism and Co-operation,
without any political and legislative reconstruction
of the State as a whole. This is the second and most
serious fallacy in his system. He ignored the fact
that such a radical change as he contemplated
could only come by legislative compulsion, which
alone could overrule the united opposition of the
existing competitive society. Voluntary and isolated efforts were powerless ; the work required the
general will of the nation, expressed in Acts of Parliament. The slow and unsatisfactory result of
Owen's agitation for the Factory Act of 1819 made
him distrust the utility of political action. He was,
of course, influenced by the fact that in his time the
people had no share in the franchise, for the Reform
Act had reached no further than the middle class.
By the time of the Chartist movement, Owen was
firmly convinced that the social evil was economic,
and that agitation for further political change was
waste of energy. In short, so clearly did he see that

Socialism was really the organization of the people to become their own masters by co-operative property and labour, that he overlooked the fact that this organization could only be effected by legislative compulsion.

Here, then, is Owen's contribution to the Socialist system : he continually, and rightly, drove home the truth that Socialism is, at root, no mere political change to a wider political democracy. There may be adult suffrage, as in the United States or France to-day, and yet no lessening of the tyranny of the rich over the poor. Socialism, he said, was the economic freedom of the people from landlords and manufacturers, not their political freedom from the Lords or Commons. It was this conception of reform as a social rather than a political change which led to Owen's use of the word " Socialism," and this has remained the universal term for the whole movement. There he left the problem, and it needed a wider mind to teach the fact that the people can only completely organize themselves by laws expressed in Acts of Parliament. Owen was the founder of conscious Socialism when he taught that it had mainly to do with the organization of industry and commerce by the people, instead of by their masters ; he was a Utopian when he taught that the people could do without political action. The right and the wrong in him were both expressed in action when he founded the communal colony of " New Harmony " in America. It was the right idea placed in a world of wrong ideas. It was putting the cart before the horse. It must not be

imagined that he had no place for political government in his Socialist State, for he conceived of the
State eventually having elaborate functions when
the scheme was perfected. He only misplaced the
order of development. The State had to take the
first step, not the colonies.

There was one point of detail in Owen's schemes
which shows how firmly he had grasped the idea
that the community is the only safe controller and
owner of any kind of capital whatsoever : he declared that the custody and education of children
must not be left to the parents, but should be in
the hands of the community and guided by its
collective wisdom. Private property was not to
cease merely in the form of land and workshops and
tools ; it must also cease in the form of children.
Indeed, Owen was a better Socialist than many
of the latter-day kind ; he understood the danger of
more than mere industrial monopoly when he wrote :
" I declare before the world that man till this day
has been the slave of a monstrous trinity : private
property, childish and irrational religious systems,
and, finally, marriage."

III

SAINT-SIMON

1760–1825

Born 1760 of ancient family descending from Charles the Great. Volunteer against England in American Rebellion. Wrote on science, and ruined himself, financially, by marriage and other social experiments. Became clerk. In 1817 wrote *L'Industrie*, his first Socialist book ; followed, amongst others, by *Nouveau Christianisme*, 1825, the year of his death. His ideas were worked out as a system by a sect of followers, the chief of whom were Enfantine and Bazard.

WHEN this descendant of the royal house of Charlemagne realized that the nations around him were in a chaotic muddle of social mismanagement, he demanded a radical upheaval and reorganization of society ; and, with a somewhat marked reversion to type, he called upon two people to lead the revolution. One was the King, Louis XVIII, the other was the Pope, who was somewhat embarrassed by a request to lead the faithful in a crusade against poverty. However, Saint-Simon quickly discovered that the aristocrats of his day, whether regal or ecclesiastical, had not the abounding energy of his own illustrious ancestor, so he lost faith in aristocracy ; and, renouncing his title of Comte, became president of his commune after the French Revolution. But it did not require much thought to understand that " the people " of that time were not more fitted to govern the country than the nobles and ladies whose gross blunderings had ended suddenly under the blade of the guillotine. So when Saint-Simon dismissed the aristocracy of blood and rank from his plans, he did not call the democracy to lead the way ; he invented a new aristocracy of scientific experts. This conception of the world under the rule of scientific officials is Saint-Simon's contribution to Socialist thought. It is, unfortunately, a conception which only Mr. Sidney Webb and a few others have properly appreciated at its full value ; and this Utopian reformer has still a lesson to teach to an age which prides itself on its advanced reformers.

To the mind of Saint-Simon, as to the minds of all who are entitled to the name of Socialist, the problem which presented itself was the proper manner of organizing the business of the community so that it should benefit the whole rather than a limited class. He had fought under Washington during the political revolution in America ; he had returned to France and seen the effect—or perhaps it would be wiser to call it the want of effect—of the political revolution there. In both cases the republic had arrived, and the real evil remained much as it was before : there was still economic waste of labour, and gross injustice in distributing what was produced. Saint-Simon had travelled widely ; he realized the possibilities of the latent wealth of the world. And the outcome of his meditations was the magnificent prospect of a world run as a business concern by the most efficient managers that could be found for the good of the whole human race. Saint-Simon had no illusions about democracy : it was not necessary to have the blue blood of Charlemagne in one's veins to be sceptical whether the fiery mobs who had engineered the French Revolution would be able to build up a new society on the ruins of the old society which they had so successfully pulled down. Whether Saint-Simon should not have set himself to the work of educating the people is another matter. He did not do so, and despotically declared that the world could only properly be ruled by an aristocracy of intellect. He could no more imagine a society where all are equal than he could imagine a workshop where all are masters. Work must be done by those who best know how to do it ; and if we want our work done well, then we must raise the expert to power and obey him : and all this for the very common-sense reason that it pays us to obey the wise man. It is easy to see why Saint-Simon took this view ; he was faced by an obviously incapable people. On the other hand, he had that unshakable confidence in personal capacity for leadership which so often exists in those whose ancestors have been ex-officio leaders for generations ; he had confidence in genius rather than in mediocrity. He was obsessed by the value of the great man. When he proposed marriage to Madame de Staël he said, " Madame, you are the most remarkable woman in the world, as I am the most remarkable man ; and doubtless our child will be still more wonderful." It is almost a picture of genius converted into a close corporation—which was far from his belief, however.

Saint-Simon's idea of government was, therefore, a body of scientists conducting the business of society in the most scientific way. When we remember that it was such material affairs as the construction of a canal from the Atlantic to the Pacific through Central America, and another from Madrid to the coast, that aroused the enthusiasm of Saint-Simon ; and when we remember, further, that Lesseps took the proposal for the Suez Canal from the same source, then it will be obvious that the Simonian great man was not to be merely a political philosopher of abstract thought (like the sentimental politicians who fill Parliament to-day), but a hard-headed man of business. As a matter of fact, the men who gathered round his·teaching had the keenest minds of the young generation ; they were men who afterwards made their names known as engineers and industrial chiefs. It is noteworthy that these people of affairs are the same who formed the somewhat fantastical guild which invited George Sand to become its high-priestess.

The Saint-Simonians, finding men unequal in capacity, drew the conclusion that therefore their power must be unequal, and likewise their reward. They endeavoured to plan a system of society which would clear the way for the great man. Of course, they appreciated the lesson of the French Revolution when it abolished the privileges of the

aristocracy of birth ; but they had discovered the
deeper evil when they said that the right of succession was " the most vital of these privileges, and
sums them all up." So the right of succession to
the property of the dead must be abolished, in order
to do away with any artificial interference with the
success of merit : every man or woman must start
equal. They also appreciated the fact that the
private master had the worker in his grip so long as
the master held the factory and the tools, so they
agreed that " the instruments of labour, land and
capital, shall be held by the united members of
society." But there was not to follow a communal
sharing of the wealth produced. Since the capacity
of the workers was unequal, they were to have pro-
portionate rewards. " Every man shall be appointed as his power befits, and paid in proportion
to his labour." In short, within the limits of communal possession of the instruments of production,
the Saint-Simonians recognized the unlimited right
of private property if one had sufficient energy and
skill to collect it.

Such was Saint-Simon's idea of the perfect state
—a community where the wise had all the power,
and also a very ample share of the produce of their
labour. And these selected leaders received their
marching orders, so to speak, in the instructions
that " the whole state should work for the better-
ment of the moral and material condition of the
poorest." The statement that the real end of
government is the performance of industrial and
commercial business by public officials, chosen for

their skill, is the gist of his teaching. It is the glorification of the expert official. It is obvious where the scheme broke down, and still breaks down, in practice. It suggested no method of putting the right man in his right place. There are plenty of wise men in the world, but neither under the rule of autocrats or of democrats do they inevitably, or even very often, get chosen to lead. Saint-Simon neither provided a way of selecting them, or of restraining them from abuse of their power, or of compelling the people to obey them. In short, he did not bring his aristocracy of intellect into organic unity with the democracy it was to govern. In other words, Saint-Simon preached the eternal truth that government is a business for skilled officials, and not for amateurs ; but he did not tell us how to find these men, and how to persuade the people to follow their advice. His conception of the State as the highest form of business organization rises to the height of poetic imagination. " The Golden Age of the world," he wrote, " is not behind us, it is before us : it is the perfection of social order." That was no vague desire, it was the expression of a man who planned canals, whose friends were engineers and scientists.

IV

FOURIER

1772–1837

Born 1772, son of prosperous tradesman. After good education entered business as commercial traveller, thereby gaining insight into industrial waste under competition. Two years in army. Published (1808) *Théorie des Quatre Mouvements ;* in 1822, *Traité de l'Association Agricole Domestique ;* in 1827, *Le Nouveau Monde Industriel.* Spent the last ten years of his life waiting for a capitalist who would finance an experiment of his scheme. Died 1837. His ideas much discussed in United States between 1840–50. About forty colonies attempted, the chief of which were Brook Farm and Red Bank.

THERE was at least one man who was quite certain that Fourier had found the real solution of the social problem of poverty. That man was Fourier himself. He sent England the tempting message that by following his scheme of co-operation for six months it could pay off its national debt out of the profits from the poultry-yards alone. But there is not much need for wonder that Fourier was an optimist ; for he had discovered, or thought he had discovered, a very comforting fact at the basis of human character. It seemed to him that men are by nature inclined to do right if their wishes are given free play : they only do what is wrong because they are restrained by the rules of a stupid system called civilization. That was Fourier's first discovery. He had, further, analysed the passions of man, and found that they are of twelve kinds : the passions of sight, hearing, and the other senses, of love, ambition, friendship, and for offspring, and so on ; and all these fit into each other with the final result of a great master passion, which Fourier named *Unitéisme*—which meant, in other words, that men are naturally inclined to club together in social groups and work together for mutual good, instead of fighting with one another under the system of competition. These two characteristics of humanity Fourier made the basis of the " phalange," or social unit, which he taught should be the framework of human society.

The phalange was to be a group of people, numbering, as a general rule, about fifteen hundred to two thousand, inhabiting land of a square league or so in extent. This area was to be worked, in agriculture and industry, by the united efforts of the whole community, acting under the direction of managers chosen by the people. The choice of each person's particular place in the group lay with the individual himself, who would be free to choose his occupation or his several occupations (for variety of work was especially recommended by Fourier) ; and he would attach himself to one of the elementary groups of seven to nine workers which formed the unit of industrial organization. This group, in turn, would unite with similar groups, until they had made up a series of twenty-four to thirty-two ; and the series would combine to make the phalange. It is obvious that the mathematical precision of this plan is fantastical, and lacking in any scientific basis. Fourier got his idea of the suitable number for the population of the phalange in the following manner : he said, the twelve elementary passions of man could be combined in eight hundred and twenty various ways ; now, since it was eminently advisable to have no gap in the social body, at least one of every possible combination should be present ; and, allowing for the old, the sick, and the immature, Fourier thought fifteen hundred a reasonable minimum. Such a precise statement of the essentials of a rational society may rightly seem ridiculous to the practical mind, which knows how human nature has unexpected kinks and fancies which upset arithmetical calculations ; but it was child's play in prophecy to a man who had estimated that eighty thousand years were the limitations of human existence, half of which time was to be spent on the upward grade and half on the way down.

Such being the framework of the phalange, Fourier worked out the details. The main structure was very similar to Owen's " township," but the details were quite different. Owen's Socialism was very thorough : property was to be entirely communal in its distribution as well as its ownership ; that is, the co-operatively produced wealth was to be shared in common, share and share alike. But Fourier's Socialism was qualified by large exceptions. After every individual, whatever his

merits or work, had been paid an ample sum for
necessaries out of the common store, private property was to exist. After the sum for necessaries
had been deducted and distributed on strictly
communal principles, the remainder was to be
divided into three unequal parts. Five twelfths were
to be allotted to a labour fund, which was distributed
on the principle of more being paid for hard or unpleasant work than for pleasant work; three
twelfths were to go to " talent," which was judged
by the rank to which an individual had been elected
by his fellow-workers; the remaining four twelfths
were to be paid as interest on the capital advanced
by private proprietors to the community. Here
we see where Fourier's system failed to reach the
complete Socialist position of making capital the
sole property of the State. But although a member
of the phalange could thus hold private capital, it
must be observed that his interest in it was the
payment of a fixed proportion determined by the
community at large; and, further, he had no
power of investing it under his own control, he
could merely place it under the complete control
of public management. The position is similar to
what it would be if we conducted our whole business
in the form of municipal trading, run by private
capital. Fourier never appears to have desired
the abolition of private capital; he did not get
beyond complete public control, though, it must be
admitted, that control was to be absolute; while up
to the point of actual necessaries, his system was
pure communism. Public control is, of course,

merely a temporary position, as it is understood to-day; but Fourier scarcely seems to have recognized this.

The phalange idea has obvious affinities with Owen's "township"; and, like Saint-Simon's, Fourier's main concern was to organize industry in the way most profitable for the whole community. They all three started from a very material point— the economical production of wealth for all. It is therefore a little surprising to learn that Fourier warned his readers of "*les pièges et charlatanism de deux sects.*" "Snares and quackery" scarcely seemed the most fitting epithets for what was so like his own. However, they serve to remind us that there were differences sufficiently great, apparently, to get on Fourier's nerves. It is not strange that a man who made the free satisfaction of the individual desires the very root of his system, as Fourier did, should have rebelled against the autocratic imposition of salvation from above, which Saint-Simon contemplated with an easy mind. Just imagine how impossible it would have been for Fourier to hope for reform at the hands of the Pope or King Louis. If any good was to come, it could only be just because the people willingly brought it about; if leaders were needed, they must be of the people's choosing. Saint-Simon dreamed of a benevolently despotic State; Fourier was not anxious for a State at all, though he did foresee a time when the phalanges of the whole world would be federated under a rather visionary Great Chief of Phalanges, who was to live at Con-

stantinople. As there were no railways or tele-
graphs then in view, he probably thought such a
far-away monarch would be fairly safe, from the
point of view of liberty. It was the same passionate
protection of the free will which led Fourier to retain
the idea of private capital, even though it was to
be controlled ; and therefore it was that he could
not reconcile Owen's pure communism with the need
for personal liberty.

This conception, both of the need of personal
liberty and also of the safety with which it may
be granted without bringing the social edifice to
ruin, is perhaps Fourier's chief contribution to
Socialist thought. The care which he gave to
protecting it in detail is suggestive of his trend.
For example, all payments of the communal share of
personal wages from the commune were to be made
to the individual, not to the parent or to the head
of the household ; thus the wife took independently
of her husband, the child independently of the
father. Again, the marriage bond was to be entirely
at will, which of course quite easily followed the
recognition of the child as an independent being,
entitled to personal dealing with the State. Both
Fourier and Owen are still well in advance of the
bulk of present thought on the subject of marriage
and the family. When we have dismissed all the
absurd fantasies of Fourier's schemes, the mathematical rules for the groups, the want of a central
government nearer than Constantinople, and so on,
there yet remains enough to entitle him to a place
amongst the leaders of Socialism. His phalange is,

after all, a first attempt to visualize the unit of organization in the Socialist state; it is a crude forecast of the modern conception of the Socialist municipality. It is, however much it may fail in details, a recognition of the fact that social organization must group itself round the requirements of industrial life; and still further that industrial life must be subject to the desires of the individual human mind. Fourier remembered that work should be a source of pleasure.

V

LOUIS BLANC

1811–1882

Born 1811, son of Inspector-General of Finance. Soon known
for brilliant journalism : established *Revue des Progrès* in
1839, in which he published his schemes. His writings
gained him leadership in the Revolution of 1848, which un-
seated Louis Philippe. The workers of Paris insisted that
he should be given a place in Ministry, and begged him to
accept the Dictatorship, which he refused. Attempted to
found National Workshops for unemployed, but they were
deliberately ruined by the Government. The workers rose
in arms once more ; were slaughtered by Government ; and
Blanc fled to England, where he wrote history. Returned
to Paris in 1870, and elected as Radical Deputy. Died 1882.

OWEN looked upon the State as a tolerable
institution, which did not count very much,
one way or the other. Proudhon thought it a quite
intolerable institution, which was a public nuisance,
to be got rid of as quickly as possible. Fourier's idea
of a central executive, if there must be one, was
to put it nowhere nearer than Constantinople.
Saint-Simon thoroughly believed in the State,
though his only attempt to influence it directly
was by an appeal to the good nature of the King.
But Louis Blanc not only believed that the State
was the main hope of good government, he took
his ideals into the heart of political affairs and

addressed a National Assembly in support of his views. In short, he made Socialism a subject for active politicians—that is his great claim to be placed amongst the leaders of his party. As a matter of fact, this honourable post of first Socialist politician was somewhat thrust upon Blanc, and he was distinctly uncomfortable. When two hundred thousand workers came to offer him the dictatorship of France, Blanc very promptly declined it. Nevertheless, willingly or unwillingly, he brought Socialism into the main stream of politics, whereas before it had been turning in a backwater. Of course, men do not do what they wish, they have to content themselves with obeying the commands of the spirit of their age ; and that autocratic voice between 1830–48 said that the next step of the Socialist party must be into the political arena if any further progress was to be made.

It was a boisterous entry which the amiable Louis Blanc found himself unexpectedly forcing into the heart of the bourgeois government. The very loftiness of the ideals of the Great Revolution made the miserably ineffectual accomplishment only the more utterly ridiculous. Bourbon, convention, republic, dictator, emperor, and back to king again, each and all made little difference to the wage-earning man ; so he began to think for himself. There had been a breath of a people's revolt in the crises of 1830, but it came too soon to have any lasting effect. The teachings of Saint-Simon had not reached the working - men, whose minds were in a state of confusion so far as any practical pro-

gramme went. Then some of them were sent to
prison for sedition, and during their year's isolation
they put their ideas into shape. (There is probably
more danger to society bred in prisons than outside, though it pleases the ruling class to imagine
it is guarding itself by sending all rebels there.)
They read the history of Babeuf's conspiracy, and
his views of government, and came out wiser men.
Then Blanc, in 1839, published a book on the
Organization of Labour. He had taken the phrase
direct from Saint-Simon, and we have here the
link between the so-called Utopians and the political
movement. This book reached the workers, and
became the text of the Socialist propaganda of
the next ten exciting years ; and it was the text
of the workers during the Revolution of 1848, as we
shall see. It was in this book that Blanc expounded
the scheme of national workshops, with which his
name is always connected, and which are generally,
but wrongly, considered his main title to fame ;
but, as already said, it was his political work which
really remains as his greatest memory. The
national workshops were an endeavour to express in
detail Saint-Simon's general ideal of the organization
of labour by the State. At the root of Louis Blanc's
scheme was the conviction that the primary duty
of the State is to guarantee to every citizen the
certainty of regular work, and it practically follows
that it therefore becomes the duty of the State to
organize work under its own control—farms for
agriculturists, factories for mechanics, shops for
tradesmen. The State, said Blanc, should imme-

diately buy the railways, the canals, the mines, and the great industries, the banks and insurance companies, so that it would be able more easily to co-operate with temporary schemes for unemployed relief. As the temporary remedy there were to be State loans of money, or the State guarantee of private loans, to groups of workmen whereby they could start workshops on their own initiative. Eventually all individualistic enterprises would be superseded by those working on co-operative principles, under the control of the State.

In this suggestion for the organization of labour there is, with all its fallacies, a definite advance on the suggestion of the Socialist leaders we have hitherto discussed. First, there is not that definite rupture from existing environment that there is in the case of Owen's township or Fourier's phalange ; Blanc's co-operative workshops, whether the temporary State-aided one or the permanent State-controlled one, were practically a substitute for joint-stock companies ; and from an industrial system of capitalist companies to one of co-operators was not a revolution so much as evolution. Secondly, Blanc insisted that it was the State which must initiate these co-operative associations, which Owen and Fourier hoped might spring up out of the people's goodwill and common sense. Further, Blanc required an overlooking State, to make such general laws for the control of the associations as might be necessary—though Owen was with him in this last particular. As a temporary remedy for unemployment in a capitalist society it is probable that Blanc's subsidized temporary workshops were unworkable and useless. As Proudhon said, they would make work for the unemployed, and take it away from the already employed; to find fresh fields for work in a capitalist society is a rather hopeless quest, seeing that unemployment usually arises from an overstocked market. But, as a description of the ultimate constitution of a Socialist society, Blanc's "social workshops" are perhaps as good a forecast as any other, and we must distinguish carefully between the temporary subsidized workshop started by the unemployed and the permanent State workshop which was to take the place of private trade. All that Blanc claimed for the former was that it would lead the way to Socialism by absorbing the workmen thrown on the refuse-heap by the capitalists, and would be a beginning in the organization of co-operative labour.

But, as we have seen, it is Louis Blanc's part in the political events which culminated in the Revolution of 1848 which gives him his place amongst the leaders of Socialism. In 1840, the year following the appearance of his book on the *Organization of Labour*, there was published a summary of the revolutionary demands : " These are our principles. We ask for a community of workers, that is to say, we desire to abolish the trading of men in the labour of men ; and, instead, to establish national workshops where the wealth produced will be divided amongst the workers, where there will be neither masters nor valets." This is the meet-ing-place of the theorists such as Saint-Simon and Fourier, and the democracy which, so far, had known no weapon but a street riot. And Louis Blanc is the connecting link between theory and democratic power ; and the result was the foundation of Socialism as a political force. This first attempt at union was—well, the first !—like most first attempts, it was crude and unsuccessful. On the people's side there was still little more than barricades and riot ; on the theorists' side there was still little more than a visionary scheme, which was more suited for Utopia than France in the middle of the nineteenth century. The police report of 1846 described the situation from the point of view of the masters : " Agitators, despairing of getting their way by purely political reform, have begun to teach doctrines which they have borrowed from the dreams of the Utopians." A government of sordid money-spinners has never yet understood the " dreams of Utopians," so the fight was desperate. The workers demanded that Blanc and one or two others should be given seats in the Ministry. They were admitted and promptly outvoted. So the workers marched into the Assembly with arms and demanded " the right to work." It was Blanc who put their demand into legislative form : " The Government of the French Republic hereby guarantees the existence of the worker by giving work to all citizens." The Assembly gave way, or pretended to give way ; " national workshops " were established, and the hours of labour were ordered to be reduced. The Government did not enforce the latter, and deliberately ruined the workshops, which were put under the control of one of Blanc's chief opponents. The men were set, in the main, to useless work, or paid wages while they remained idle. It came out in a Parliamentary inquiry that the Government deliberately intended to make these " workshops " an organization of degenerate men, who would fight against the serious workers if these revolted. Suddenly, when the Government felt itself strong enough, the sham workshops were dissolved. The indignant democracy rose in arms, and was crushed out by main force. Blanc was accused of leading the revolt, which he had not done, and fled to England. So the first attempt of Socialism to enter politics failed.

VI

FERDINAND LASSALLE

1825–1864

Born 1825 of wealthy Jewish family. Disliked business, and
studied philosophy and politics at universities. His brilliant
talents gained him entry into literary circles ; the admired
of Humboldt and Heine. Of private fortune, he devoted
himself to fashionable life and democratic agitation. In
1848 worked with Marx, and exiled from Berlin for sedition.
In 1861 wrote *System of Acquired Rights*. In 1862 revolted
from Liberals, and asked by workers to draw up a programme
for them ; which he did in the *Open Letter*, which led to
the foundation of the Universal German Working Men's
Association in 1863, the beginning of German Social Democracy. Killed 1864 in a duel arising from a love affair.

I T was the unforeseen destiny of a smart man-
about-Berlin-town, famed in his set for elegant
appointments, to succeed before any one else in
laying the foundation of a workers' party as an
organized political force. To Louis Blanc belongs,
we have seen, the honour of being the first Socialist
to bring the movement into the current of active
political life. But he went there somewhat against
his will, and the followers behind him were only an
incoherent body, useful for little else than popular
demonstrations in the streets. Lassalle, on the contrary, marshalled his army for the parliamentary

battle because that work was the essence of his being. He saw that the next step was the organization of the workers as a fighting political force ; he was conscious of a great power of accomplishing this, for the man of fashion was deadly in earnest when he said that the world was for the labourers, and that he wanted to lead them to their lawful rights. Not only did he go into politics with a conscious joy—whereas Blanc hesitated—his work was permanent, while Blanc's was rather a suggestion than an accomplishment. Since 1863, when Lassalle founded the German Working Men's Association, there has been a Social Democratic Party in Germany. Of course, it has developed in policy as well as numbers, until Lassalle would scarcely recognize the great organism which follows Bebel to-day as his own grown child that was born in 1863. Yet so in fact it is ; and Lassalle's great work for Socialism was the foundation of the German Social Democratic Party as the first organized Socialist political force. He began the organization of a political army which could wield the economic weapons that Marx has made for its use. Of course, Marx had already, in the Communist Manifesto of 1847, gone further than a theoretical statement of the Socialist programme, for he had said there that the workers must unite for a political attack on their masters ; for in that way alone could they seize the instruments of production into their hands. But the Communist League, and even its successor, the " International," political though they were, got little beyond theory. A league which had its origin in Paris and its central executive in London, but whose main object was the education of Germany in the principles of social reform, could scarcely get to grip with the fine details of the business of practical politics.

Lassalle put into practice what Marx and others had taught as a principle. They said, " Workers of the world, unite." Lassalle actually began to unite them. It is very important to observe one reason for his success. He started with a national ideal : he tried to organize a German nation of workers ; he had no particular sympathy with the dreams of a united world—or perhaps it would be fairer to say that he sacrificed Utopia for the victory of to-day. Lassalle believed in the necessity for a united Germany, and to that end he welcomed the supremacy of Prussia, which he saw was the only possible bond of union. He accepted the monarchy. He went a good deal further, he accepted Bismarck, who, by the way, said that this founder of the Social Democratic Party would be an ideal neighbour to hold the next estate to his country seat. So that Lassalle set out to found a Socialist Party in Germany, not to unite the workers of the world long before they showed any longing to be united.

In Germany, however, the moment was opportune, the fruit was getting ripe, and Lassalle obeyed his destiny (which is the destiny of all great men) by plucking what was ready to his hand. He came into the current of politics at the moment when the Prussians were fighting for a constitutional assembly to take the place of an autocratic govern-

ment. In the rebellious year of 1848 he stood
beside Marx and made his first confession of faith :
" Gladly do I avow that, from the impulse of my
nature, I am on the side of the Social Democratic
Republic." He was so impatiently on that side
that he planned an insurrection, and until 1859 he
was banished from Berlin. But he had not yet
clearly distinguished between the sham reform which
the Liberals meant by a democratic constitution
and the real reform of society which he had in his
own mind. However, he soon saw that the Liberals
were a broken reed, and it was in 1861 that he began
to sever his connection with them. It is of the
greatest importance to appreciate the position of
the Liberal, or, as it was usually called, the Pro-
gressist Party, at the moment when Lassalle declared for leaving it. It had gained a majority in
Parliament ; it was now at last in a position to
fight the Crown with a plausible chance of victory ;
it included in its ranks advanced men, who were
practically Socialists in their opinions. Lassalle had
been co-operating with this party during the days
of its struggles, now it seemed only fair and wise
to give it time to try its strength. At this moment,
of all others, Lassalle bursts forth into an almost
savage attack on " Liberal bourgeoisie, whose conception of politics is one of supine dullness and
superficiality " : they fight " about words, with
words, for words." Then, in 1862, he took a
further step : he appealed to the workers direct,
in a lecture before one of their clubs. He told them
that the State was a mighty machine for the over-

coming of poverty and chaotic mismanagement of
society ; while the Liberal bourgeoisie thought it
was only an instrument for protecting life and
property—" a night watchman's idea," said Lassalle, with withering contempt. Then followed one
of those highly strung phrases which gave Lassalle
his power over men : it was the destiny of " the
working-class estate " to lead all others, for they
were the State itself. " The vices of the oppressed,
the idle indifference of the thoughtless, even the
harmless frivolity of the small-minded, no longer
become you now. You are the rock upon which
the Church of to-day must be built." The State
replied promptly by prosecuting Lassalle for in-
citing the poor against the rich—which was, indeed,
a capital summary of his intentions. The defence
was pure brilliancy, and the end of the trial was a
small fine. In June of this same year Lassalle
wrote to Marx the significant sentence : he had
" begun a little practical political agitation."
Then the workers, discontented with the futile
result of Liberalism, asked Lassalle to propose a
plan for more effective action. He replied in the
Open Letter (1863), which has been named the
" Charter of German Socialism."

It contains the essence of Lassalle's leadership,
and it still stands as a model of alluring persuasion
and close reasoning. He tells his readers that they
are in the grip of an " iron economic law." They
come into the labour market to sell their only property—their labour power ; and they get paid for
it at the market price, which, like the price of other

goods, is fixed by the competition between the applicants for work. So that the wages are driven down, under the law of competition, to the bare cost of maintaining life at the standard of the day and reproducing its kind. " This is the limit within which the wage swings like a pendulum, without much exceeding it, or falling far short thereof." There are some who would have us believe that this " iron law " is a thing of the imagination, and that the laws of competition can be, and are, evaded in all sorts of ways by the worker when he bargains with his master. Such criticism overlooks the fact that Lassalle admitted that the price must rise (or fall) with the current opinion of what " maintenance " should include. So far as current opinion is with him, the wage-earner can demand a higher standard of maintenance ; but at the best he gets nothing better than that—and mere maintenance is not life or justice. So Lassalle said : " This iron and cruel law you must before all else grave in your hearts, and make it the beginning of all your thought." " Your share of wealth is always the bare necessities of life ; your master takes all the rest."

Then follows this conclusion : If the masters always win the bargain, the " iron law " must somehow be evaded, by putting the workers in a position where there will be no need to bargain with masters at all. So Lassalle expounded his scheme of " productive associations," or, as we should now call them, co-operative production societies, where the wage-earners were to work for their own profit

instead of for capitalists. Now whether these
associations were either sound Socialism or practical
politics is a doubtful matter; though it is important
to bear in mind that Lassalle advocated them as
nothing but a transition stage on the way to complete collectivism. They were only, in his judg-
ment, the best temporary, practical step. They
are almost of a kind with Louis Blanc's suggestions,
and are equally open to criticism in several aspects.
But their intrinsic value is not the important point.
It is because they led on, as in Blanc's scheme, to
the demand for State assistance, that they must be
mentioned in an account of Lassalle's work for
Socialism. For there followed the pregnant conclusion that the workers, if they needed State aid,
must put into office a government which would
grant that aid. What sort of government would
do this? Here was the critical point. Did the
political parties, whether autocrats or progressists,
want to abolish the " iron law "? " If," said
Lassalle, " the man who talks of the working class
acknowledges this law, then put to him this further
question—how does he propose to abolish it? If
he has no answer, then turn calmly your back on
him, for he is an idle chatterer." The Liberals
had no answer, so the workers must turn their
backs on them and organize a party of their own.
The workers to whom Lassalle addressed himself
agreed, and he set to the work of organizing his
independent political army. We must keep clearly
in mind that he was breaking new ground, and that
he only lived rather over a year after he began the

work. The General Working Men's Association
was founded in May, 1863, and in August, 1864,
he was killed in a duel which he fought for the hand
of an adventurous lady, whose haughty family
refused their consent to her marriage with such a
social rebel as Lassalle. But he lived long enough
to set an example of political agitation of which, it
would seem, we scarcely yet know the art.

He put his views before his hearers in clear-cut
sentences ; he divided the theory from the practice ;
so that there could be no confusion of ultimate
ideals with temporary expedients. The first step
in their plans must be universal suffrage ; but he
drove it home that this was only in order that they
might clear the way ; in itself political reform was
valueless. But as it was a necessary step, let them
use their full energy in taking that step. " The
whole heart of practical success consists in concen-
trating one's whole force at any time on one point."
Therefore their independent union was to be announced as formed for the obtaining of universal
suffrage. It was to be presented as a " bread and
butter " question, on which their material welfare
entirely depended. Lassalle forgot no method by
which they could carry their message into " every
workshop, every village, every hut " : newspapers,
trusts, paid agents, clubs—he even remembered
the value of songs—all these means were to be
concentrated on saying " daily, unwearyingly, the
same thing, again the same thing, always the same
thing." He made public agitation a fine art ; he
realized that in one way or another the people

must be worked to the pitch of enthusiasm. When he had ridden into one town under triumphal arches and half smothered by flowers, he wrote: " I felt that such things must have happened at the birth of new faiths." He had mastered the secret of touching the people's imagination; he used his art to separate the workers from their false friends and to start them in an independent way of their own.

That was Lassalle's great contribution to Socialism: he founded the art and practice of translating Socialist theory into political action. His co-operative associations were probably a mistake, even as a temporary expedient. His Workers' Party, clear cut from all other parties, was an epoch-making event in the history of the movement.

VII

KARL MARX
1818–1883

Born 1818, son of Jewish lawyer holding high post in Civil
Service. Brilliant university career in philosophy and
history. In 1842 began revolutionary journalism; so
effective that paper suppressed by Government. Went to
Paris, where met Engels, 1844. Lifelong friendship with
him: together drew up " Manifesto of the Communist
Party," 1847, which the Communist League adopted as its
programme. This may be called the foundation of modern
Socialism. Returned to Germany to help revolutionaries
in 1848. Returned to London, 1849, where he lived the
rest of his life, engaged in working out and writing down his
Socialist teaching. First volume of *Capital* published 1867 ;
the other two volumes appeared after his death. Also took
active part in the affairs of the International Association of
Working Men, until its end in 1873. Died in 1883.

ONE writes down the name of the greatest
figure in Socialist history with a sense of
very real reverence, for, criticize him as you please
or as you can, when all is said he yet remains the
leader of leaders. Whether you think of him as
scientific economist or as practical politician Karl
Marx stands first and alone, a colossus of thought
and action. When one searches about for some con-
cise way of expressing just what this great man accomplished for Socialism—or, to put it the other way

round, when one wants to measure the damage Marx
did to the ranks of the enemies who oppose Socialism
—by an almost weird paradox (although the biggest
things in life are usually paradoxical), there seems
no manner of summing him up quite so near the
truth as in eight lines from the most famous of
comic operas :—

> " The criminal cried as he dropped him down
>   In a state of wild alarm,
>   With a frightful, frantic, fearful frown
>   I bared my big right arm ;
>   I seized him by his little pigtail,
>   As on his knees fell he ;
>   As he squirmed and struggled and gurgled and guggled,
>   I drew my snickersnee."

That, in brief, is exactly the Marxian method of
dealing with the Capitalist theory. He chopped
it up. With ruthless precision, strangely com-
pounded of calm scientific curiosity and a more
elementary delight at the sight of blood, Marx
placed his victim piece by piece on the dissecting-
table. There was a total absence of the modern
anæsthetic in the Marxian method. Indeed, it is
a mistake to use a surgical simile at all. Marx did
not dissect the Capitalist system, he tore it limb from
limb, battered in its body. Or, if you insist on
hiding the real result under gentler words, then one
can say with Mehring that the Marx and Engels
" workshop was not a spinning-room where the
peaceful wheels revolve with a monotonous purr.
Rather was it a smithy, where sparks flew all around
under the crash of the great hammers with which

they were forging the mighty weapons of the proletarian Class War."

Until Marx spoke there had been a vagueness about the purport and end of Socialism—whence it came, what it was, and whither it was going. When Marx had written *Das Kapital*, had drawn up the " Manifesto of the Communist Party " for the Communist League in 1847, and had guided the International Working Men's Association until its end in 1873, people might say they did not believe in Socialism, but they could never again say that it was not possible to understand it. Hitherto Socialism had been based on sound humanitarianism, but on shadowy economics. Marx formulated the whole movement in one clear issue—the Class War between Capital and Labour, with the collective control of industry as the necessary and inevitable issue, the only solution of the evils of society. The older Communist League had for its motto, " All men are brothers." Marx said that was not so : men were either capitalists or wage-earners, and there was endless war between these two classes in the existing society, and must be war because their interests were irreconcilable. So long as there were employers at all, there must inevitably be wage-slaves to serve them. What the one gained the other must lose, there could be no mutual gain. So Marx preached the great Class War. His Communist Manifesto closes with words which are historical ; indeed, they are more than historical, they are burning words to-day : " The Communists do not seek to hide their opinions and desires. They say clearly that their end can only be gained by a violent overturning of all social organization as it exists now. So let the masters tremble at the coming of the Communist revolution. The workers have nothing to lose but their chains ; they have a world to win. Workers of the world, unite." This conception of the whole Socialist movement as a struggle between the man who buys labour and the man who sells it—that a man is either an exploiter of some one else's labour or exploited by some one else—that is the fundamental truth at the very root of Socialism which was not understood until Marx made it clear as day. It is still possible to find antediluvian minds who cannot see the full significance and truth of this generalization of men into two economic classes. There are, of course, individuals who are on the border line (there are doubtful species in all departments of natural history), and those whose minds are more conscious of the trivial exception than of the almost universal law will continue to remain blind to the greater economic fact. It is especially in England that an attempt has been made to explain away the Class War, and to soften it into vague and unscientific phrases which will not admit that there is any definite economic distinction between master and servant, except a matter of indefinite degree. The result is that, not having taught this basis of Socialist theory, we in England have not yet succeeded in making Socialism understood by the people as it is on the Continent, where the Class War is taught as the essential basis of the movement.

This fundamental conception of the Class War Marx expounded as a scientific deduction from economic law and historical fact. He took Socialism up as a generous sentiment; he put it down for all who followed him to accept (or fear) as an inevitable, scientific certainty. In so far as it is possible to summarize his teaching it can be placed under three heads. There is no need to claim that Marx owed nothing at all to his predecessors. No man is original, he only takes the next step, he only develops what others have said or done; and so with Marx. But some men develop more than others; Marx went so far that his next step seemed a revolution.

It is first necessary to grasp the importance of what Marx expounded as the " materialist conception of history." He meant, briefly, that the course of historical development is governed primarily by economic facts, and only in a quite secondary degree by political or moral or religious facts. In other words, men do this or do not do that, because such a course of action, or inaction, is best adapted to the industrial, or agricultural, or commercial requirements of the day. That is, all social systems are governed by the need of producing most easily the necessities of life. Society is really governed by the laws of manufacture, agriculture, and trade. As Engels puts it : " The materialist conception of history starts from the principle that production, and next to production the exchange of its products, is the basis of every social system. . . . The ultimate causes of all social

changes and political revolutions are not to be
looked for in the heads of men, in their growing
insight into eternal truth and justice, but in changes
of the methods of production and exchange ; they
are to be looked for not in the philosophy, but in
the economy of the epoch in question." For example, we gave up the slave system not because we
thought it inhuman, but because the slave-owners
found the wage system more economical. When
we had discovered that slavery was uneconomical,
then we discovered that it was inhuman. Progress
is governed by the laws of political economy. Marx
brought down politics from the airy realms of vague
sentiments, and translated political problems into
the terms of material loss or gain. It was by teaching that society is ultimately governed by the production of bread and butter that Marx stands as
the leader of the politics of Reality, and has stamped
Socialism as the doctrine of practical affairs, leaving
its opponents as the preachers of sentiment and
romance.

Such being Marx's conception of the basis of
history, the materialist basis, his next contribution
to Socialist thought was to show that Socialism is
coming to pass not because people consciously
strive for it and hope for it, but just because it
must come as the next step in natural evolution.
Primitive communism, production by slaves, feu-
dalism with its serfs, the medieval yeomen and
craftsmen, the age of the Elizabethan merchant
adventurers, the industrial revolution, which manu-
factured paupers and millionaires at the same time—

all these systems, passing from one into the next, were the result of a mighty law of social evolution, against which it was useless to struggle, had any one wished. The urgent impulse to proceed with the business of creating wealth drove mankind from one system, as it became old and unsuitable, to another which was possible under modern conditions. And now the Capitalist system is, in its turn, becoming impossible, rapidly tending to chaos instead of organization. So it will pass into something better ; and the next step is to social co-operation, or collectivism. Marx proved that Socialism is just as inevitable as every other phase has been—just as much beyond the control of those who fear it, or of those who deny it. Since Marx expounded the laws and facts of historical evolution, we Socialists can take the haughty stand that we are the expounders of nature ; we can taunt our enemies that they are vainly waving their arms and wagging their tongues in a childish attempt to turn back the destiny of the ages. The Capitalist is weaving his own shroud did he but know it. The Utopians had marshalled to their aid the forces of humanitarian goodwill. Marx placed the laws of science at the disposal of Socialists. He wrote : " Their work could have no tenable theoretical basis except that of a scientific insight into the economic structure of society, and that this ought to be put into a popular form, not with the view of carrying out any Utopian system, but of promoting among the working classes and other classes a self-conscious participation in the process of historical transformation of society that was taking place under their eyes." Marx said, and proved, that Socialism is part of the " historical transformation." He besought men, as it were, not so much to work for Socialism, he rather begged them to be conscious of it, to meet the inevitable with open eyes.

The third great work which Karl Marx did for Socialism was to analyse the Capitalist system in its domestic details, to find the place of Capitalism in the social order.   In his materialist conception of history, in his statement of the laws of historical evolution, he always had the great fact of Capitalist production in the front of his mind.   It was in his work on *Capital* that he went behind the enemy's lines, so to speak, and came back with plans and information which laid the opponent's position open to the first army of organized Labour which had wit enough to attack.   He tore out the secrets of the employer's methods by the very roots : it was the most ruthless investigation which the world has seen.   He tracked Capital to its den ;   he demonstrated that the rich man's wealth came from one single source—the labour of his wage-slaves.   The Capitalist paid his men just enough to maintain them in a tolerable, or intolerable, state of existence ; sometimes did not even pay that, so that the sweated slave died off prematurely, and was replaced by another.   These servants worked all day producing " value."   A quarter, a third, a half, perhaps two-thirds of this " value " which they had created was returned to them as wages ;

the " surplus value " (i.e. all that remained over
after the wages were paid) was seized by the master.
After the analysis of Marx there can be no doubt
as to the verdict against Capital. Proudhon had
already declared that " property is robbery," Marx
proved it by scientific reasoning. He proved that
Labour, physical or mental, alone creates value.
Capital is value which the master takes, by economic
force, from the men who created it. In short, Marx
seized the master " by his little pigtail " and branded
him as a thief. Of course the victim " squirmed and
struggled and gurgled and guggled," declared that
his capital was " the reward of abstinence," " the
rent of ability," legitimate interest or profits, or
some sweeter sounding name than " robbery."
It may even be admitted that Marx's theory of
value will not fit every exceptional case : it may
not explain the value of potatoes during a famine,
or the value of a " first edition," or the value of a
house in Park Lane ; but in ninety-nine cases in
a hundred the Marxian snickersnee reaches the
heart. As Engels said : " The theory of surplus
value struck home like a thunderbolt out of a
clear sky."

The work of the greatest man in Socialist history
was to place Socialism on an unshakable scientific
basis. Compared with this, his active political
life was less important. And yet he gave German
Social Democracy a programme ; he practically
founded the International Association, which, as
the International Socialist Conference, still is the
link between all Socialists. He was, and remains,

E

the inspiring spirit of all militant Socialism, since the day when he wrote, in the Manifesto of 1847, " the first step in the revolution by the working class is to raise the proletariat to the position of the ruling class, to win the battle of democracy. The proletariat will use its political supremacy to wrest, by degrees, all capital from the bourgeoisie, to centralize all instruments of production in the hands of the State." In short, as a scientist and as a practical political thinker, Marx is the father of Socialist thought and action. He showed that Socialism is the decision of science ; he showed that the wage-earners must work out themselves the salvation of society.

VIII

H. M. HYNDMAN

Born 1842, son of wealthy barrister. Educated Trinity College,
Cambridge. War correspondent and journalist in early life.
Founded Social Democratic Party in 1884. Parliamentary
candidate at Burnley, 1895 and 1906, but unsuccessful
because he always tells the whole truth. The writer of innumerable pages of Socialist literature : *The Historical Basis
of Socialism, England for All, The Economics of Socialism,*
etc. Innumerable speeches.

I F the Liberal and Tory Governments really had
power to do what they would like to do, and
could pass an Act of Attainder whereby all our
Socialist leaders were condemned to be tied in the
same sack (it would be an exciting sackful) and
lowered into the sea ; if, just to confirm the repeated
statement that they have no real ill-will towards us,
the Governments said we might choose out one
amongst the victims to receive pardon and release,
and if a popular vote were taken as to whom should
be saved, then, if we were wise, we should choose
Mr. H. M. Hyndman. If all the rest were to be
swept away, it would be supremely important that
the sole survivor should carry the gospel tradition
in its purest form ; it would never do if the future
Socialism were to spring forth again from some
diluted source, which had been contaminated with

compromises and surrenders and temporary aberra-
tions. After all, there is only one Socialism, in
theory or practice : the man who preaches and
practises that to the last word is a Socialist, and
whoever stops short is by that so much the less a
Socialist. So that if one wanted to save Socialism,
instead of some transitory deduction therefrom,
then we would do well to pray that Mr. Hyndman
be spared out of the sack. When one describes
the rest of the leaders as " Socialists," there always
seems need for some further qualifying phrase ;
one is a tactician, one a scientific economist, another
a craftsman, another a philosopher, this one a
Utopian, the other a wire-pulling parliamentarian.
Mr. Hyndman is just a Socialist, and if you do not
like his Socialism you can leave it ; or, rather, you
must fight it, for there is no other.

It has been Mr. Hyndman's mission to build in
England the central citadel of Socialism, while
others have engaged (often quite successfully and
usefully, be it remembered) in unauthorized raids
and risky adventuring into the enemies' ranks. He
has defended the citadel, while others have been
defending (often very wisely defending) outposts
and detached companies. If all the adventures
failed, and the outposts were all cut off, the real
army would be quite untouched within the walls,
and ready to strike when the time came for warfare
instead of border raids. One inevitably falls into
military metaphors when writing of the leader of
the Social Democrats, for his conception of the
fundamental change which Socialism must bring

into the existing social organization is so vivid, that
he cannot conceive of it coming to pass without a
terrific fight—whether it will be a physical fight
or a political one, he candidly confesses he does not
know. The bare, fundamental structure of Socialism, without gloss or qualifications, with all its
inevitable conclusions drawn without an attempt
at concealment, the truth, the whole truth, and
nothing but the truth (so help him, Marx), such is
Mr. Hyndman's contribution to Socialist thought
and practice. It is a work which no one else in
England came forward to do, and it was work
which most urgently needed to be done.

The English mind, apparently, is too lazy to grasp
general principles ; it occasionally can rise to a
detail here or there ; but a clear view of an important whole seems beyond its vision. Mr. Hyndman himself holds that the Capitalist system has
degraded our working class, by sheer hard work,
below the same classes on the Continent, just because
in England that system has been developed more
ruthlessly than elsewhere. However, whatever may
be the reason, in England it is peculiarly hard to get
the ordinary man, who rules in these democratic
days, to grasp what Socialism really is. The
vision of the complete whole, which alone can make
it intelligible, and alone can make it ardently
desired by the people, is lost to the English sight.
In so far as he thinks about it at all, the Englishman
conceives of Socialism as a gradual tinkering with
details, without any radical alteration in the general
system. It is confused with that estimable principle

" Social Reform," which is the pet of every politician according to the urgency of his need for votes on polling day. Some of these reforms are good enough in their way ; but, at the best, they make an infinitesimal difference in the condition of society ; and they are totally useless as an inspiring war-cry to rouse the people to the great effort which alone will bring Socialism. In short, there was, and is still, in England an imminent danger that Socialism may be conceived of as something little better than Social Reform ; and that, in so far as that is any good, it will be won in the same ways and by the same political parties which have won it in the past. Socialism would, on this theory, be handed over to the good pleasure of Liberals and Conservatives who do not want it ; instead of being committed to the care of a Socialist party which will fight for it and adopt it on every occasion with the whole force of conscious determination. Mr. Hyndman founded the Social Democratic Party because he saw that at all cost, of political expediency or anything else, Englishmen must be taught that Socialism is a change in fundamental principles ; that it is not a gradual extension of Liberalism or Tory democracy, or any such juggling with the Capitalist system ; that it is the entire upheaval of that system, which can only be brought about by a violent political warfare (if it comes to nothing worse) against the supporters of Capitalism.

Against him and his methods were all the little minds which could not see the whole ; the impatient minds which insisted in getting tiny in-

stalments ; the simple minds which imagined that
the Liberals or Conservatives would gradually give
Socialism if they were encouraged by Socialist
support. Against all these Mr. Hyndman defiantly
hurled the challenge that he was out to fight for
Socialism and nothing short of it ; he was out to
abolish the wages system, and nothing else was any
use, or of so little use that it was not worth any
compromise with the enemy. He told the Trade
Unionists that they were " devoted to the wages-
system " ; he told the co-operators that they
merely " yearn after dividends." As for the masters
themselves, there was no mincing of words about
them. Mr. Hyndman said in round English that
they were robbers and unscrupulous slave-drivers.
When other reformers (who would have been more
happily placed in a Sunday-school) were preaching
to the workers patient waiting, and telling the
masters that they were in the grip of a vicious
system and not really to be altogether blamed,
Mr. Hyndman declared for the Class War in words
of the bitterest invective ; and it may safely be said
that not one of his adjectives was undeserved.
The fight was between " the Park Lane gang "
and the people whom they robbed in the form of
profit, interest, and rent. He told the masters that
they have inherited " most of the bestial qualities
of their forbears," who slaughtered little children
in mines and mills during the early years of the
industrial revolution. To take note of all the
groups which lie between Park Lane and the wage-
earner, is to lose sight of the essential fact in a mist

of trivial details. So Mr. Hyndman pitted the
robbed against the robbers, the worker against the
capitalist ; clearly said that it was a fight to the
death between these two great classes ; that there
would be no reform worth the name until the
worker had annihilated his enemy ; that Socialism
would alone destroy the masters, while Trade
Unionism and Co-operation and that vague mystery
" Reform " did not matter in the least.

The Class War and Socialism, from first to last.
That is Mr. Hyndman's message. In a crowd of
wire-pullers, compromisers, Labour men, Fabian
men, timid men, and crafty traitors, he cleared a ring
for the Social Democratic Party ; and there was one
platform where the laws of Socialism were expounded
to the last word. It is worthy of notice that this
Social Democratic faith is stricter than the Marxian
itself. Marx was content with Labour alliances ;
and he was right in thinking that they were safe in
Germany, where the workers are capable of grasping
the real position so clearly that they could make
concessions and yet not lose sight of the real
point of their aim. But Mr. Hyndman knew
England better than Marx ; he knew that we are so
prone to compromise that we cannot go that way
without infinite risks of straying so far that we never
get back to the main road at all. Compromise
may not be wrong in every case ; in the case of the
alliance between the Independent Labour Party and
the Labour Party it may be, at present, well advised.
If so, it has been safe just because the Social Democratic Party has stood firm. The Independent

Labour Party has been possible just because the Social Democratic Party preaches what, for the present, is impossible ; the Independent Labour Party could safely make terms with the Trade Unionists just because the Social Democratic Party mounts guard over the Red Flag. The Independent Labour Party could be Marxian because Mr. Hyndman took the responsibility of being stricter than Marx. He has been the subject of gross misrepresentation ; he is entitled to comfort himself with the thought that the Socialist Party in England will one day take the place of the Labour Party ; and when that happens it will be discovered that the real Socialist Party and the Social Democratic Party are one and the same thing. For the Social Democratic Party has stood for Socialism and nothing else ; which is exactly what a real Socialist Party will do.

IX

SIDNEY WEBB

Born 1859. Educated London University (LL.B.), Switzerland,
and Germany. Clerk in War Office ; Surveyor of Taxes
(1879–81) ; in Colonial Office (1881–91). Called to Bar,
1885. Lecturer on Economics at City of London College.
Elected to London County Council, 1892. Has written, with
his wife, a series of works of the highest value in historical
and sociological science : *History of Trade Unionism*, 1894 ;
Industrial Democracy, 1897 ; *Problems of Modern Industry*,
1898 ; *English Local Government*, of which three large volumes
have appeared. Senator of London University, and Chairman of the Governors of the London School of Economics.

ONE cannot easily believe that violent revolutions will ever happen in this sleepy England ;
so we have decided (somewhat hastily, perhaps),
that revolutions are unscientific. Nevertheless,
one of these days, after a course of better feeding
and shorter working hours, it is just possible that
even an English mob will forget its respect for
science, and will do something rash. If it so happens,
when the first messenger fights his way out of the
rabble to carry round the great news of victory
(we will assume that, for the moment), it will be
interesting to hear how the leaders of Socialism
receive his tale. " The Social Revolution is accomplished " he will shout. Mr. Bernard Shaw, in the

confusion, will forget that he is a Fabian, and will wave an imaginary shillelagh round his head, as befits an Irishman. Mr. Hyndman and Mr. Keir Hardie will have heard the news already. But Mr. Webb will say : " The Social Revolution ? I scarcely expected it. So it is really over. Then we can begin, at last." The reader must note that word " begin." It will seem a damp, unappreciative word to the messenger who has seen the last reactionary chased down Pall Mall and heard the last shot fired which cleared " law and order " out of Whitehall. " Begin, indeed ; it is ended," he will pant with indignation. But Mr. Webb already will be on his way to take charge of a Department in Downing Street, where he can get to the work of " beginning " Socialism. He cannot think of a successful rebellion bringing Socialism any nearer ; for in his mind Socialism can only come by an infinitely careful attention to an infinite number of points of detail. Socialism is the organization of society, and there can be no organization by a street riot.

Indeed, if Mr. Webb were told that Socialists had won—not merely a physical battle, but had captured every parliamentary seat and were in possession of the Houses of Parliament, and had swamped the Lords by raising Mr. Quelch and his friends to the peerage—Mr. Webb would still say : " Ah, then we can begin." Revolutions, either military or political, cannot bring Socialism ; for that can only come by organization of the smallest details with the greatest pains. It is all a matter of administration, of putting into working order schemes which, however scientific, are only Utopian until they are actually in practice. Any Parliament could pass a law ordering the whole land to be nationalized, or the railways, or the bakers' shops and the coal mines, the telephones and the cycle trade. But it would be a matter for ceaseless thought and experiments to find out how best to cultivate the land ; how to run the trains for the public good rather than for the good of the shareholders ; how to bake bread, dig coal, arrange telephone wires, turn out cycles in the best possible way for the public advantage ; that is, for the advantage of the whole people. In short, the organization of industry under the State will be no less a matter of careful business detail than it is under private control. Indeed, it will need infinitely more care ; for it is only the profit to the masters with which private enterprise is ultimately concerned, whereas State industry must be undertaken for the good of the whole people, whether producers or consumers. The problem before Downing Street under Socialism will be the production of the greatest amount of wealth, in the most convenient way, and its distribution to the people in accordance with the laws of equity and social utility. When Mr. Webb starts off for Downing Street after the Social Revolution, he will ponder that he is going to take charge of a bankrupt business which must be reorganized from top to bottom ; all his work will be before him. Vague ideals, lofty aspirations, generous sentiments, will not help him or his fellow ministers when they sit at their desks and write instructions for their subordinates. Only a precise knowledge of the facts and a clear idea of how to deal with them will make Socialism a working system instead of a Utopian desire. The thing which weighs on Mr. Webb's mind is the immensity of the problem before us and the depth of our ignorance. He has written, in 1894 : " I am appalled when I realize how little attention we have yet been able to pay to what I may call the unsettled questions of democratic administration." He beseeches us " to work out the detailed application of Collectivist principles to the actual problem of modern life." Nothing is any good at all until the fine points of administration are properly settled.

Take the case of an Eight Hours Act; it is the simplest thing in the world to draft an Act which says " no one shall work more than eight hours in any one day or more than forty-eight hours a week." It is a grave problem to draft a scheme which will make that virtuous principle an accomplished fact. They have had regulation of the hours of labour in France for three-quarters of a century ; but these regulations have not got much further than the statute book. In practical life they have been almost a dead letter, because they could not work out the details so that the masters (and the men, for that matter) could not evade them. We shall have exactly the same difficulty in England. It is easy to put Factory Acts on the statute book ; it is the most difficult thing in the world to devise machinery which will ensure their enforcement.

Then again, take the case of unemployment : it is useless to say " set the poor to work " unless you can suggest the kind of work which will be suitable for the odd collection of men who will apply to the local authority. When the State can organize labour for all, that will be Socialism. The problem is how to organize it. Mr. Webb probably conceives of Socialism as a sort of Chinese puzzle where you have to fit all the little bits together. He listens to his comrades heroically declaring for the nationalization of everything; he entirely agrees with them. Then he gets a bucket of water and pours it in the form of precise questions on the heads of these red-hot enthusiasts. When the steam has cleared away he demands, " By all means nationalize everything, but begin somewhere, and come, let us consider how we are going to do it." Mr. Webb is the wet blanket of the Socialist movement. Rodbertus said he thought we should get to Socialism in five hundred years ; but Mr. Webb has not given us even that hope ; there are so many details to think out. To all our passionate hopes and demands Mr. Webb answers with the chilly question : " Yes, but how shall we do it ? " It is his contribution to the Socialist movement to have asked that question more often than any one else, and to have so often answered it as well.

He is so careful about details because he is sure that Socialism is coming by a process of instalments. He entirely disbelieves in sudden revolutions ; he thinks that social organization will, very gradually, grow more and more complete, but it will never be

possible to say exactly when the old system has
gone and the new has come. Mr. Webb, if one
reads him aright, teaches that Socialism will slowly
develop out of the capitalist system. There will be
no sudden break. There will be more and more
control exercised over the master by the State until
one day the much-controlled master will realize
that he is merely the servant of the State. His
wages list will be fixed by a Minimum Wage Act,
his factories will have to conform to the requirements of stringent Factory Acts, his profits may be
seized by a graduated Income Tax. Trade Unions
will continue to protect the interests of the workers
in their particular trade. Trusts will continue to
develop, though here and there they will quietly
pass from the unified ownership of Mr. Rockefeller
to the ownership of the State. In short, Mr. Webb
is a true Marxian in his belief that Socialism is the
inevitable outcome of social evolution. He only
leaves out the great revolution which Marx was
inclined to put in his programme at first, but did not
afterwards insist on as an essential thing. So that
Sidney Webb shares with Karl Marx the honour of
proving that Socialism is inevitably bound up with
social development, a part of the social structure.

Marx puts more emphasis on the destruction of
capitalists, Mr. Webb thinks more of the protection
of the labourers. There is no lasting satisfaction
in destruction, it is merely a negative good ; the
only finality is organization of something better.
Mr. Webb is everlastingly preaching that the problem
of Socialism is the organization of labour by the

most careful attention to an unending number of details. And to think these out is Mr. Webb's business for Socialism. He is the quencher of all enthusiasms ; the heartless arouser from all arm-chair dreams.

Now there is nothing to be gained by denying the danger of this kind of leadership, even though one admits its many advantages. " It behoves all true believers to watch and wait and diligently equip themselves for a warfare which must neces-sarily be harassing and protracted," he tells us. We are, it seems, always to be preparing for a war which will never begin. But it does not do to mistake the arsenal and the intelligence depart-ment for the seat of war ; the fighting does not take place in these retired spots. There comes a time when the battle must begin, when we must form a Socialist army to use the Socialist ammunition. At least, that is the general opinion of every Socialist association in Europe ; rather, of all but one—the Fabian Society, and the Fabian Society is Mr. Webb. Mr. Webb does not believe in fighting for Socialism. He thinks it will come most quickly by perpetual arbitration with the enemy. He thinks we should always " settle out of court," however hard the terms are. The Fabian ideal is " permeation," that is, never fight ; if you cannot talk your opponent over to your side, then give way. It is impossible to ignore this side of Mr. Webb's leadership, and to carefully distinguish it from his theoretical side. He is the only great Socialist leader who has so completely severed his theory and his practice.

In his grasp of the details of Socialism he is probably
first ; in his political practice he has thrown in his
lot with the enemies and has deserted his friends,
because he sincerely believes that it is better to
permeate opponents than to found an independent
army of one's own. So Mr. Webb went into
the London County Council as a " Progressive,"
and is quite content that a large number of the
Fabians should be warm supporters of the Liberals,
or even Liberal members themselves. He is perfectly satisfied that Progressives, or Liberals, or
Tories should get the credit if they adopt any
of his Socialist schemes ; and he does not apparently
much mind if the people at large confuse Socialism
with advanced Radicalism or Tory Democracy or
County Council Progressivism. Nobody has the
slightest objection to the enemy doing our work
for us, only we are beginning to be ambitious
and to think that we could do our work still better
ourselves. Mr. Webb, by infinite cleverness, has
undoubtedly linked the Socialist movement with the
practical politics of the day ; he has gone far towards
giving Socialism a footing in the administrative
machinery of the State and municipality. But that
method has its definite limitations. It is not always
an advantage to get a foot into machinery. The
Fabian policy of wire-pulling has been successful
in many ways ; but we must never forget that it
has been successful at the price of foregoing the
foundation of a Socialist Party. Sooner or later
we shall have to found that Party. Even to-day
we have a Labour Party which is Socialist in all but

F

name.   Mr. Webb would be the best of leaders for
such a party ; but he has chosen, so far, to think
that Liberals and Conservatives are sufficient to
give us Socialism, and is apparently indifferent
whether we have a party of our own or not.   He is
quite content that Liberals or Conservatives should
reap the credit if they adopt his wise schemes,
whereas he might get them all put down to the credit
of the Socialist Labour Party if he would only take
a place at its head.   He stands alone amongst the
leaders of Socialism in ignoring the necessity for an
independent political organization.   He is satisfied
to aim, for the present, at a national " minimum,"
which he apparently thinks will not be beyond the
intelligence of a Radical or Tory Cabinet.   He is
content to sacrifice the strength of a political attack
in, order that he may obtain the few scraps of
Socialism which can penetrate to the intelligence
of anti-Socialist politicians.   He ignores the supreme
advantage of having an army behind when one asks
the enemy for terms.

J. KEIR HARDIE

Born 1856. Worked in coal pit from eight until twenty-three. Discharged and black-listed in 1879 for organizing miners ; made secretary of their union. On staff of *Cumnock News*, 1882 ; founded *Labour Leader*, 1887. Left Liberals and founded Scottish Labour Party in 1888, and candidate at Mid Lanark in parliamentary election of that year ; was unsuccessful, but elected for West Ham, 1892, and for Merthyr Tydvil in 1900 and 1906. Took chief part in foundation of Independent Labour Party in 1893. Chairman of Labour Party, 1906–8.

WHAT the fashionable dandy of Berlin did for German Socialism when he laid the foundation of an independent political organization of the workers, a coal miner did for the workers of Great Britain. Keir Hardie, to all outward show, is everything that Ferdinand Lassalle was not : in everything that is essential the two men are as two peas. Their message to the great community of Labour was almost word for word the same. There is no hope for you but Socialism ; there is but one way of reaching your goal, the way of staunch isolation from Liberalism which is merely tinkering with the problem of social reform. The man who spent his odd moments in giving the daintiest of supper parties and the man who defiantly went to

the House of Commons wearing a cloth cap, stand
back to back fighting for the Worker against his
master with exactly the same weapon in their hands
—independent political action.   They approached
their platform from very different sides, and it is
Keir Hardie's side we are concerned with now.

That cloth cap in the House of Commons was no
insignificant detail ; it was the summary of his
deepest thought.   It is only the unfortunate
fact that one wears a cap at the wrong end of the
person, which prevents one calling it the basis of
Mr. Hardie's system.   He is what he is, and has
done what he has done, because he has been driven
forward by a great passionate sympathy for the
misery of the world ; and, being a poet (and
therefore a man of commonsense), instead of a
sentimental stockbroker, Hardie has tracked this
misery to the most definite cause.   He has tracked
it to want of food, of clothing, of housing,
of the benefits of civilization.   And the chief
victim is the wage-earner, whose rescue from misery
is Keir Hardie's passionate life-work.   When he
entered the House of Commons he did not go to join
any of the political parties who were there ; he went
solely to stand for the man of the cloth cap, who was
worth a party to himself, who must have a party of
his own if his claims were to be heard amongst the
din of sentimental fictions which passed for reality
in the Houses of Parliament.   " Humanity has the
first claim," wrote Hardie, " and the first demand
of a human being is for bread. ' Man shall not live
by bread alone.' We know and feel the truth of

the saying more fully than most persons. But bread first. Make such provision as will give food to the hungry and clothing to the naked, without demoralizing them, and then go on to higher things. But this must be the foundation on which the higher life is built." He went to Westminster with an intensely practical end in view : to give food and clothing and shelter to every member of the community ; and he was driven there because that elementary political programme had not entered into the mind of any one yet in Parliament. To the sane intellect of such as Keir Hardie the law-makers were either idle dreamers who had lost all touch with real life, or they were arrant rogues who were protecting their own interests under the guise of public service. Legislators were prating of preserving the Constitution, enlarging the Empire, protecting the Church, guarding property, while in Keir Hardie's mind hammered the awful insistent thought that (in his own words) " the tramp, tramp of the strong man out of work never ceases, and strange thoughts are beginning to find lodgment in the brains of these men who find themselves left to starve because that pays the employer."

Now, Mr. Hardie began his career as a Liberal and his supreme work for Socialism has been to tear all serious reformers away from the Liberal Party and to rally them in a new third party. The history of that change is the history of his claim to be the founder of political Socialism in Great Britain, and his actual accomplishment was the creation of the Independent Labour Party in 1893.

The Social Democratic Federation under the leadership of H. M. Hyndman, and the Socialist League under William Morris, had led the way, and done the spade work by educating the Englishman to understand that Socialism is something essentially different from the Social Reform which is the heroic cry of both Liberals and Tories—a laborious undertaking made infinitely harder because it had to struggle against the picturesque tactics of the Fabian Society which confused the plain issue on every possible occasion. But the Social Democrats and the Leaguers alike failed to reach the imagination of the ordinary citizen, which must be reached before a movement can arrive at the stage of practical politics. The movement had to wait until a man was found with a very unique collection of virtues. At last the Fates discovered Keir Hardie, poet, but also shrewd man of affairs ; the people's own man, but also the cosmopolitan who knew neither distinctions of class or race. One can imagine the wild warfare of conflicting elements which had to be settled before this man became a coherent being. The gods, without doubt, sent Hardie forth as a poet ; it is only incomprehensible fate which has made him a politician, almost the sanest politician in England.

He had seen more than one attempt to form a workers' party. In 1874 the Trade Unionists had turned against the Liberals on the question of a new Trade Dispute Act ; but they had fought without a clear programme, and the movement soon was reabsorbed in the powerful Liberal ranks, and things

were as bad as ever. Then, in 1882, came the Social
Democratic Federation, with an undue swing of the
pendulum in the opposite direction ; for its programme was so uncompromisingly clear that it
did not seem to touch practical politics at all, so far
as the short-sighted man in the street could see.
Then, in 1888, the uncompromising Socialist and
the young Trade Unionist found common ground
in the Dock Strike, which, in Mr. Hardie's own words,
" may be taken as the starting point of the new
Labour movement." The result was the foundation
of the Independent Labour Party in 1893. Its
founder has described the basis thus : " Inspired by a
Socialist ideal, they yet manage to keep their feet
firm on solid earth ; and the politicians learned that
the British workman, despite his well-known pro-
clivities, could be a practical kind of idealist when
properly led." In the Independent Labour Party is
contained Keir Hardie's life-work. First, it is a
party which preaches that the Social Reform of
amateur politicians will accomplish nothing worth
getting, and that Socialism alone is a sure remedy.
Secondly, it announces from the housetops that both
the Liberals and the Tories have been tried and found
woefully wanting, and the real reformers must form
their own army and fight for their own hand.
It is one of the mysteries of life that any sane man
can think that either the Liberals or the Tories, as
they stand to-day, are a sufficient medium for serious
reform. It was Keir Hardie's mission to preach
sanity. He had seen Governments come and go,
and the sum-total result was about the same—

nothing.   He sat in a Parliament with the overwhelming Conservative majority of 1900 ; now he is
sitting in front of the overwhelming Radical majority
of 1906, and outside " the tramp, tramp of strong
men," seeking in vain for work, goes on ceaselessly.
His mission is to open the eyes of his fellows to the
hard fact that if they wish for progress they must
march there themselves, for other politicians have
played them false.   " It makes one incredulous,"
writes Mr. Hardie, " when one hears Labour men
boast that they are using, or are going to use,
Liberalism to achieve Labour reforms.   The spectacle of a small community of kids in the midst of a
horde of wolves, comforting themselves with the
belief that they are about to use the wolves for their
own advantage, would not be more absurd."
But it must be remembered that it is the leaders who
are the danger.   " If the Liberal Party were the rank
and file the advice to trust them would be all right.
But they are not the party.   These are the crutches
on which the real party leans for support.   It is the
interests of the landlords and the capitalists who are in
the party which decide its policy."   The rank and file
may be perfectly sincere in their demand for progress ;
they are only foolish in expecting to get it from a
Liberal Cabinet.   Indeed, Hardie has a sublime contempt for the Liberals ; he will scarcely give them
the honour of being a real party.   They are merely
a senseless block in the road.   " The business of the
New Party is to do battle with Toryism.   Before it
can get to close quarters with the forces of reaction
it must first clear from the path the impediments

behind which Toryism shelters itself. The chief
impediment is the Liberal Party." That is Keir
Hardie's contribution to Socialist thought in England : the advice that true reformers must push
the Liberal Party aside without delay ; for it is
the chief " impediment " in the way of Reform.
It was on that basis that he founded the Independent Labour Party. He demands Socialism, and he
knows that the Liberals and Tories will not grant it.

XI

BERNARD SHAW

Born in Dublin, 1856. Came to London, 1876, and wrote
novels (*The Irrational Knot, Cashel Byron's Profession*, etc.),
and pictorial, dramatic, and musical criticism in *Saturday
Review, The World*, and elsewhere.   1884, joined Fabian
Society, which he has since used as his Socialist background.
Wrote two of Fabian essays, 1889 ; *Quintessence of Ibsenism*,
1891 ; *The Perfect Wagnerite*, 1898.   In 1898 began the
publication of the series of brilliant plays : *Plays Pleasant
and Unpleasant, Three Plays for Puritans, Man and Super-
man, Major Barbara*, etc.   The creator of Andrew Undershaft was once a borough councillor in St. Pancras.

KARL MARX taught that the basis of the
Socialist movement was to be found in the laws
of a strictly scientific political economy.   Lassalle
said that the way to victory was by the road of
energetic political action.   Sidney Webb said it was
all a matter of careful attention to details in administration.   But the people at large were dis-
appointingly callous to the words of wisdom ; they
candidly preferred sentimental commonplace to
scientific economy ; they refused to give up football
and horse-racing for politics ; they would not bother
their heads with details so long as any officials could
be found who would run their departments on vague
generalities.   The position became really serious ;

there was a danger that the Socialist movement
would collapse, for the scientist, the politician, and
the expert were rejected by an overwhelming
majority. There was one man who kept his head in
the moment of peril and saved a stampede ; he
got up quickly on his tub and announced that
he was an Irishman of rigid middle-class origin.
The people shouted with delight at this paradox ;
they knew there were no middle-class people in
Ireland, only peasants in the country, car-drivers
and Fenians in the towns. Then Mr. Shaw—it
is impossible to conceal any longer the identity
of the hero—said he quite agreed that the crowd had
good reason for being dissatisfied with the previous
speakers, more particularly with Karl Marx. It
was only by a gross slackness on the part of his
(Shaw's) ancestors that Marx had got his innings
first, when he could easily have been made ridiculous
at the end of his first week, and Europe would have
been saved fifty years' wanderings in the desert of
surplus value and Social Democratic pig-headedness.
But then, speaking broadly, the whole course of
history had been a blind groping in the dark until
1884, when the Fabian Society began to get things
into order. They could dismiss, as entirely unimportant, everything that had been said about
Socialism so far. There was only one basis for
Socialism, and that was the basis of commonsense.
That was the gospel that he had come to preach—
stern, uncompromising commonsense. He again
reminded them that he was an Irishman, and therefore without illusions or hasty impulses or hot-

headed emotions ; but just a man who saw things as they really are, not as romantic Englishmen and Scotsmen dream they are. And all the time the people are dancing with glee because here is, so they think, the most brilliant clown they have ever heard.

But the real humour of the situation—or the tragedy of it, if you care to put it so—is that Mr. Shaw is desperately in earnest. He really is talking sheer commonsense, it is practically the whole gist of his message ; he does it more brilliantly than any one else ; and the audience does not miss one scrap of the wit and sparkle, it claps its hands in the hope of getting more. It does everything possible to show how it appreciates Mr. Shaw, except believe that he means what he says. When he says something that cuts like a knife, so that even the thickest-skulled can understand that there is no joke there, then it is entered to the author's account as a cynicism. That is the summary of the public estimate of Mr. Shaw—three parts a clown and one part a cynic. The real man is one half a scientific sociologist, one half a poet, one half (it is quite impossible to get G. B. S. into two halves) a fiery propagandist, and all the rest of him the only living man who cannot be taken in by mock heroics and mock morality and mock—mankind. He can see through more brick walls—whether they encircle the Cabinet Council, the Municipal Council, the Ecclesiastical Synod, or the domestic hearth and its accompanying lares—than any one else ; and the result of his somewhat ruth-

less investigations into these various institutions he
has published to the world as a gospel of commonsense. It is his contribution to the Socialist movement, for Mr. Shaw has conclusively shown that
commonsense and Socialism are exactly the same
thing, and everything else is nonsense. It is the
Shavian form of the Class War. The Marxians say
there are two classes, masters and slaves ; Shaw
proves that there are only Wise or Stupid people.
He will scarcely even admit that any one is wicked
or dishonest, it is all a matter of being intelligent or
silly.

See things as they are, and get rid of all " romantic
illusions," is Mr. Shaw's first and last advice to the
world. Look life full in the face as it really is, and
don't pass along in a misty atmosphere of fine
sentimental phrases which do not touch real life at
its remotest corner. There is all this glib talk of
putting down crime and setting up virtue ; and
the stupid man, walking in his sleep, takes his
measure of crime from the code they use in police
courts, and his standard of virtue from suburban
villas. What is Mr. Shaw's measure ? " The
greatest of evils and the worst of crimes is poverty.
. . . All the other crimes are virtues beside it. . . .
Poverty blights whole cities. . . . What you call
crime is nothing ; a murder here and a theft there ;
a blow now and a curse then : what do they matter ?
They are only the accidents and illnesses of life ;
there are not fifty genuine professional criminals
in London. But there are millions of poor people,
abject people, dirty people, ill-fed, ill-clothed

people." And the fool worries his head about the fifty and leaves the millions unheeded. The sentimentalist prattles about the happiness of a virtuous conscience, to which Mr. Shaw replies that the first essential of happiness is to have " money enough for a decent life and power enough to be your own master." " I wouldn't have your conscience for all your income," says the tramp in *Major Barbara* to the millionaire. " I wouldn't have your income for all your conscience," replies the millionaire. That is the advice of the Grand-Master of Commonsense to the poor : there is no virtue worth possessing if you must take poverty with it. The unfortunate thing is that the audience at the Court Theatre who listened to the play had already made up its mind on this point, especially the people in the stalls: no man or woman with over a thousand a year has any conscience left worth mentioning. But if the Fabian Society would invest its income in a travelling company to tour round the slums of England with *Major Barbara*, and free seats, then very quickly would it be seen that the Shavian philosophy ranks beside the Marxian in the Socialist system ; and, as a method of propaganda, beats it hollow. Here is Mr. Shaw's summary of his gospel : " Idealism, which is only a flattering name for romance in politics and morals, is as obnoxious to me as romance in ethics or religion. In spite of a Liberal revolution or two I can no longer be satisfied with fictitious morals and fictitious good conduct, shedding fictitious glory on robbery and starvation, disease, crime, drink, war, cruelty,

cupidity, and all the other commonplaces of civilization . . . our persistent attempts to found our
institutions on the ideals suggested to our imaginations, by our half-satisfied passions, instead of on
a genuinely scientific natural history."

That is the essence of Mr. Shaw's message :
throw the fictitious code of manners and morals
and political institutions into the waste-paper
basket, and draw up another code founded on
scientific principles, based on the facts, not on the
sentimental fancies, of life. This gospel he preaches
with an indescribable energy and earnestness, with
the remarkable result that the most serious thinker
of the day is usually described as its prince of
jesters. People sit before him in rows at the
theatre, or in the circulating library, or the daily
papers' correspondence columns, shrieking with
laughter at everything which Mr. Shaw thinks
solemnly true and sacred. Has this light-headed
audience ever taken the trouble to read this jester's
estimate of his patrons ? " The hysterical, non-
sense-crammed, fact-proof, truth-terrified, unbal-
lasted sport of all the bogey panics, and all the
silly enthusiasms that now calls itself ' God's
Englishman.' " " The intellectual laziness and
slovenliness of the Englishman is almost beyond
belief." " That hero-worship of dotards and duffers
which is planting England with statues of disastrous
statesmen and absurd generals." · Mr. Shaw's plain
talking to Englishmen is that they are utterly
foolish persons, who are outwitted at every turn.
They think they are paying for statesmen and

generals who know their business, and can give value for their salaries ; and, instead, they get men who are running the Government and the Army on the principles of a sentimental school-girl. When these foolish persons ask to be allowed to keep Ireland in the scope of their British management, Mr. Shaw turns on them savagely (as savagely as the gentlest-mannered man in London can turn) and asks them to read Mr. Booth and Mr. Rowntree and the health reports on English slums and English starvation, and cease this silly chattering about the right of England to govern Ireland, when it is unable to govern London or York or Manchester decently. The foolish person says England should govern Ireland by right of empire, or some other heroic sentiment. This commonsense person says there is only one test of right—do you know how to govern ?

Thus Mr. Shaw puts every question to the test of cool-brained, level-headed thought, and the sum-total result is the same as the teaching of Marx and Jaurès and William Morris—it all comes to Socialism. Shaw states it in terms of common-sense instead of in terms of political economy or of politics or of art. He once wrote a book which he named *The Commonsense of Municipal Trading ;* the preface says : " There are no figures in this book. . . . The balance-sheet of a city's welfare cannot be stated in figures. Counters of a much more spiritual kind are needed, and some imagination and conscience to add them up, as well." There you have Mr. Shaw's work ; it is a series of shrewd balance-sheets of the affairs of life " with some imagination and conscience to add them up."

There is one dark mystery about G. B. S.'s life, a strange contradiction which is continually cropping up in his words and acts. He has all the marks of the natural-born rebel, who takes the strong independent line just because he cannot help going that way. It seems impossible to imagine Bernard Shaw coming to terms with any party but his own ; it doesn't seem possible that he can stand anywhere except out in the open of the field, whole yards away in front of the first fighting line. One can only think of him as a solitary figure, who can get no one to keep pace with him. That is the Shaw of all departments of life but one—and it is a very big exception. In every other circumstance Mr. Shaw's great joy it is to ride full tilt against the foe and tear him ruthlessly limb from limb. In politics he does nothing of the sort : he hides away with the Fabian Society in the rear, perpetually talking of compromise and gentle permeation, when every man is needed in front with a gun. That is where Mr. Shaw stands in the rear with the Fabian Society ; and yet (this is the mystery) at odd moments, even in politics, he makes rushes towards the fighting line ; odd sentences get written, such as : " No fact has been more deeply stamped into us than that we can do nothing with an English Government unless we frighten it." Or this one : " It has been said that the French Revolution was the work of Voltaire, Rousseau, and the Encyclopedists. It seems to me to have been the work of men who

G

had observed that virtuous indignation, caustic criticism, conclusive argument, and instructive pamphleteering were as useless as praying. Eventually, as we know, perfectly respectable citizens and earnest philanthropists connived at the September massacres because hard experience had convinced them that if they contented themselves with appeals to humanity and patriotism," etc. . . . " I, who have preached and pamphleteered like any Encyclopedist, have to confess that my methods are no use. The problem being to make heroes out of cowards, we paper apostles and artist magicians have succeeded only in giving cowards all the sensations of heroes, whilst they tolerate every abomination, accept every plunder, and submit to every oppression." That is how Mr. Shaw speaks when he is on his own. Then he gets lured back to the Fabian Society, and he writes " Fabian Notes " in *The Clarion*, where he tells you that Mr. John Burns was quite right to give up trying to frighten the Government, that he was right in ceasing from February riots in Trafalgar Square, that he was eight, in short, in entering the Cabinet so that he might give political cowards the sensations of rarnest reformers, while they tolerate every abomination (see above). By some strange process, in the domain of politics Mr. Shaw throws over every principle which he preaches in other spheres of life. It is very mysterious. He seems in the grip of a powerful influence which coils round his mind ; one thinks of the tale of Svengali, who was, if we remember rightly, a dark man with a pointed beard, of weird hypnotic influence. Every now and again Mr. Shaw will make a dash for freedom ; there are rumours of an independent Socialist party ; but all this heroism comes to nothing, and he is soon sitting obediently on the Fabian plat-form, preaching the virtues of permeation ; and one wonders if his Svengali is near him then.

XII

JEAN JAURÈS

Born 1859. Professor of Philosophy at Toulouse. Elected to Chamber of Deputies, 1885–9, when he sat as Moderate Republican. Became a Socialist. When re-elected in 1893 he rapidly became leader of the Socialists by reason of his extraordinary combination of brilliant oratory, tactical skill, and great intellect. Has written a History of the French Revolution, and many articles in his paper, *L'Humanité*, and elsewhere.

IF one compares Ferdinand Lassalle or Keir Hardie or H. M. Hyndman with Jean Jaurès, it is hard to see at the first glance how they can both claim to be leaders of Socialism ; for on the surface they have done quite contrary things. Each of the former three strove to present Socialism as a separate and isolated force, working on its own lines, for its own hand. They threw their whole force into the attempt to detach Socialism from an alliance with Liberalism, or Progressivism, or Social Reform. They tried to bring about a state of affairs when every one would be either a Socialist, working inside a Socialist Party, or an enemy working against that party. Such was the broad effect of their leadership (the case of the Independent Labour Party's alliance with the Trade Unions is a passing detail beside the general principle of isolation), and there are few careful students who will deny that their doctrine was urgently needed in the circumstances which faced them. Then, if the work of Jean Jaurès is drawn in the same broad outline, it seems that he must be praised because he has attempted (and with success) to link Socialism with all the varied sides of life, to show that it is necessary for the solution of every problem ; that it is not an isolated thing, but can only rise or fall as an intimate part of the whole social structure. Now, it must not be imagined that Lassalle and Hyndman and Hardie overlooked this intimate unity between Socialism and Society at every point ; they only preached isolation because that was the only way of getting people to understand the difference between the real remedy and all the quack remedies which were being expounded by quack reformers. Then, when there had been clear demonstration of the essential structure of Socialism and comparative safety from any confusion with other methods of reform, it became the time to re-blend the detached principles with the whole social problem, from which they had been necessarily but, in a sense, artificially withdrawn. It has fallen to M. Jean Jaurès, the most powerful and the most picturesque of living Socialist leaders, to play this part in the evolution of the system. It is altogether important to realize that although it has been Jaurès' particular work to illustrate the unity of Socialism with the whole political and social problem, yet there has been no sacrifice of the clearness of the Socialist position. Jaurès is a great enough man to take his creed into daily life without allowing it to be soiled.

After all, Jaurès and the French Socialist Party are the creatures of their circumstances. The Social Democrats of Germany find themselves in a Parliament which is under an unconstitutional monarchy. The German Government is not appointed and controlled by the Reichstag, but is under the immediate orders of the Emperor. An adverse vote in the Reichstag does not displace the defeated ministers, who can be dismissed by their imperial master alone. A few Socialists, in a house where even the majority does not govern, never enter the sphere of practical administration, but stand outside as onlookers who cannot go beyond criticism, without power to enforce their verdict. In the French Parliamentary system the position is very different. The verdict of the French House decides the fate of the Government ; to convince the Chamber of Deputies is to convince—nay, it is to order—the men who are governing France. The French Socialists are therefore face to face with the problem of governing France ; not merely, as their German comrades, faced by the possibility of criticizing an absolute emperor's way of governing. For the Socialists in France are now an appreciable part of the democracy ; they have an appreciable share of the seats in the Chamber of Deputies ; they have three of their men in the Cabinet. Such is the position in France, and it gives the key to M. Jaurès.

When he found himself in the most democratic country in the world, the greatest orator and the most accomplished statesman, and a real power in the state, he grasped the fact that he could not hold

himself apart from an individualist society. Strictly
speaking, Socialism is an economic doctrine, dealing
with economic facts and only touching other sides of
life in so far as all life is based on the production of
material necessities. But when the Socialist finds
himself a national statesman, it is borne on him that
he is the teacher of a creed which has no limits
to its compass. The theory and practice of Socialism
are so interwoven with the tissue of life that they are
one and the same thing. Jaurès, in a masterly
essay on French History, has been showing how
even the Kings gave their country unity; how the
bourgeois Revolution gave it a kind of political
liberty; how wise the proletariat was when it
refused to listen to the absurd advice given by those
who, like Marat, animated by the spirit of class,
said: "'What are you doing? Why are you going
to seize the Bastille, whose walls never imprisoned
a working man?' It marched to the attack,
determined the success of great victories, rushed to
the frontier, saved the Revolution at home and
abroad, became the indispensable power, and
gathered as it went the prints of its incessant
activity"; how Saint-Simon and Fourier entered
into the spirit of the new industry instead of fighting
it blindly. Then he, Jaurès, bursts forth with his
summary of it all: "Everywhere, then, Socialism
is a vital force, moving in the direction of life itself,
and in its fiercest current. . . . No, Socialism is
not an academic and Utopian conception, it is
ripening and developing in closest touch with
reality." That is the great thought which runs

through everything Jaurès does and says: he refuses to admit that Socialism is only an economic question ; a thing apart from an unreformed world ; an outside element which will have no power until the great Social Revolution comes. To Jaurès Socialism is part of the present life " and in its fiercest current."

The effect of this conception has been very far-reaching in Jaurès' leadership. It is scarcely an exaggeration to say that he forced the Socialist Party to lead the demand for a revision of the Dreyfus trial. He said that justice and liberty were essentials of his faith ; they might not be economic problems ; they were Socialist problems, however (that was a challenge to narrow sectarianism). Then, again, he led the attack against the Church. While the German Social Democrats take a strictly impartial position regarding religion, Jaurès is responsible for the fact that Frenchmen have almost banished religion from their country. The question is not an economic one, perhaps ; but it is the duty of intelligent men to crush out forces of superstition and reaction which stand in the way of the freedom of the mind. It is possible to argue that Jaurès fought so fiercely against the anti-Dreyfus party and against the Church party because they both aimed at the restoration of the monarchy. That may be so in a degree ; but even then the safety of a Republic is not, strictly speaking, the business of a Socialist who is out for economic changes only. German absolutism and American democracy are, on the face of it, much the same to us, because they are the same to the capitalist. But both Pope and King were in the current of life as Jaurès saw it. They had to be conquered, with many other outposts, on the way to the economic enemy. Then, once more, we find this leader of the French Socialists in the thick of the debates on the Morocco War, in possession of military information before even it reached the Government, just as he had been the first to publish news from Rome which made the ecclesiastical separation of 1906 inevitable. In short, Jean Jaurès is not only the first Socialist in France ; he is also rapidly becoming its first statesman. It is day by day more possible that France will make him Prime Minister—not because she desires Socialism, but because she wants the present system managed to the best advantage. There is something masterly in the way in which Jaurès has made his followers take their place in the front of the national life in every aspect of it ; and yet has never allowed the main principle of their party to be obscured. He and they became anti-clerical, anti-militarists, or pro-Dreyfus, without letting it be forgotten that they were, above all, Socialists.

Now, the wide reach of this national outlook is the inevitable outcome of Jaurès' conception of what Socialism involves and demands as its basis. Again and again he reiterates that Socialism is for the whole people and can only come through the whole people : " it is the party of all the people with the exception of two hundred thousand great proprietors, small proprietors, bourgeois, and priests."

There is one way only of reaching the Socialist State, and that is by making the great bulk of the people Socialists. By no subterfuge or sharp political practice can the government be captured ; for, after all, it is not merely the Cabinet which must be won, it is the whole community which must be prepared for the change. " There is only one sovereign method for Socialism—the conquest of a legal majority." " No trick, no machinery of surprise can free Socialism from the necessity of winning over the majority of the nation by propaganda and legal method." That is the conviction of Jaurès, and he accepts the inevitable and sets himself to convince the majority that there is not one corner of the social field outside the vision of the leader of French Socialism. And further, Jaurès holds that there is not going to be any violent moment when Individualism will cease and Socialism begin. He accepts the theory that we must proceed by evolution and not by revolution. " A Society as complicated as ours is not revolutionized by a popular rising of a few days, but by an immense continuous effort of organization and transformation." Why, Mr. Sidney Webb might have written those words : they might be put in the Fabian Basis.

But note how this evolutionary theorist becomes a revolutionary when he enters the domain of politics. Had he been a Fabian he would have wormed himself into the Chamber of Deputies as a moderate reformer, hoping that the next step would be dragged a little further if he got one end

of the political wire which worked the machine.
But Jaurès, the most accomplished wirepuller and
parliamentary strategist in Europe, does nothing of
the kind. He goes into the political arena as a
militant Socialist. Clemenceau may profess, and
with all sincerity, that he is aiming at the same
end as the Socialists, and that he is prepared to take
all practical steps on the way. Jaurès' answer
is to fight this Reformist Government at every opportunity, in the polling booth and in Parliament.
On the other hand, when he considered it necessary
to save the Republic from a monarchical reaction,
he formed a temporary *bloc* with the Republicans.
It is the consummate skill with which Jaurès has
formed temporary alliances, and has yet maintained
his independence, that is his invaluable lesson to the
Socialist movement. He has stated the problem
thus : " I acknowledge that this complicated
policy which I am trying to formulate before the
party, a policy which consists in at once collaborat-
ing with all democrats, yet vigorously distinguish-
ing oneself from them ; penetrating partially into
the State of to-day, yet dominating the State
of to-day from the heights of our own ideal
—I acknowledge that this policy is complicated,
that it is awkward, that it will create serious difficulties for us at every turn, but am I to suppose
that you ever hoped, with your deep practical feel-
ing and high intelligence, that you could pass from
the period of capitalism to the organization of
Socialism without coming across these difficulties
incessantly ? " There you have summed up the

whole problem which it is the destiny of Jaurès to
state, and, in large part, to solve. He has kept his
Socialist faith a clear-cut thing ; and at the same
time he has entered into the practical government
of a capitalist state, so that it may be worked for
the best of a bad result and prepared for its transformation into something better. Jaurès admits
the necessity of compromise with the enemy; but
there must be no surrender of the main position.
Thus, when Millerand, a Socialist, took office in a
Liberal ministry, Jaurès objected : "he, consciously
or unconsciously, abraded and blunted overmuch
the sharpness with which the proletariat should
stamp its own force and will, even on the democracy.
That is what I blame in his policy ; that is its
danger." In short, Jaurès has changed Socialist
politics from the inflexible theory of the study to
the bold practice of everyday life.

It was one half of his work to link Socialism with
the current life of his country ; the other half has
been of equal importance. Jaurès found the elements of probable and possible Socialism in France
scattered into innumerable groups : ranging from
rigid Marxians to the vaguest of trade unionists.
The Socialists were split into all possible shades of
theory and practice ; the Labour associations were
anything from anarchists to timid benefit societies.
Before there could be any successful battling with
the capitalist enemy, it was clear that there must
be some form of unity evolved out of this chaos.
Jaurès saw the element of good in each body,
strengthened that element and almost ignored the

bad. It is interesting to read now some words which were written in 1895: " Citizen Jean Jaurès, a sincere Socialist, and one of the greatest orators of French literature, past or present, has maintained a position of complete independence." From this position of isolation he is gradually, by a process of infinitely skilful balance of forces, gathering together in one united Socialist Party all the chaotic elements of real reform. Marxians, Reformists, General Strikers, Class-warriors, and Class-unconscious folk are slowly closing the ranks for united parliamentary action against the men who are out to defend capitalism.

The gist of the work of Jean Jaurès has been to smooth away all the differences which keep Socialists apart ; to accentuate all the distinctions which separate them from the supporters of Individualism ; to bring together this conflict into a great parliamentary battle ; to persuade the majority that Socialism is a practical policy for a modern State and that it does not ignore one single essential problem of life. He is, in brief, the most advanced leader of Socialist theory and practice that we have yet seen.

XIII

WILLIAM MORRIS

1834–1896

Born 1834. Educated at Marlborough and Exeter College,
Oxford. Articled to architect, but did not continue, and
spent his life in producing a monumental mass of works in
every department of Art. Founded Morris & Co., decora-
tors ; also the Kelmscott Press. Wrote many books of
poems—*The Earthly Paradise*, etc. ; many prose works of
romance. Saw that Socialism was necessary as the foundation of culture, so threw himself into the Socialist movement
with terrific energy in the early eighties. Died 1896.

> " Dreamer of dreams, born out of my due time,
>   Why should I strive to set the crooked straight ? "

SO William Morris had written of himself when
he was a young man. In his fiftieth year,
this " idle singer of an empty day " suddenly threw
on one side his poetry and his craftmanship, which
had made him famous throughout Europe—nearly
neglected them for seven years, in an almost frenzied
attempt to teach his fellow-men the economic and
political doctrines of Socialism. The result of
those seven years' work has been to place Morris
with the leaders of Socialism; to place him, indeed, in a unique position among them. And he
comes near the end of the list because his teaching

carried the theories of the movement to a farther point of thought than any other of the master-Socialists had reached. It was no mere flight of fancy on his part, a passing holiday in the land of Utopia. Morris's contribution to Socialist thought was just as solidly constructive and as unanswerably scientific as the work of Marx. Like most real poets, Morris was a man of keen practical mind, who got deeper below the surface of things than the men whose lack of imagination drives them into the Stock Exchange and the counting-house. He was, in the real sense, a man of business, the producer of commodities, and he saw quite clearly that this work of producing commodities must be, for the great bulk of people, the main business of their lives. Since this was so, he saw that it was infinitely more important that a man's work should be so arranged as to be itself a happy thing, rather than that the working hours should be times of driving and congestion in order that the play hours should be longer. For, when "labour-saving" machinery has done its best (or worst), the work of producing the necessities and managing the business routine of our lives will still probably remain the chief concern of our waking hours. Therefore, when Morris saw that the Socialist's business was the organization of labour by the State, he saw that the matter in hand went far beyond the organization of a system which would get the work done in the shortest time and in the most economical manner. For in exercising control over the greater part of men's

active life, the community would be making or
marring their hope of happiness.   If the work done
and the manner of doing it were not productive of
happiness or tolerable contentedness, then men's
lives must be passed in unhappiness and discontent.
Therefore the Socialist's problem of the organization
of labour was nothing more or less than the organization of happiness and a joyful people.

Morris was first and foremost a craftsman ; to
him the essence of life was the making of the most
useful products in the most beautiful way.   Life,
in his eyes, was a time to be passed in enjoyable
work ; and there was only one way of doing that,
namely, by having leisure enough to do sound, and
therefore beautiful, work instead of being rushed
into turning out from the workshop what was
merely cheap.   This grasp of the basis of sound
living made Morris a Socialist ; for the capitalist
system was clearly capable of producing nothing
but shoddy goods and half-starved, overworked
labourers ; it was not a matter of prophecy ; it
was blank, staring fact.   Morris saw the fine possibilities of the world " muddled away by the greed
and incompetence of fools who do not know what
life and pleasure mean, who will neither take them
themselves nor let others have them."   And the
first craftsman of the day flung down his tools,
and spent his days and nights in the attempt to
knock down this colossal monstrosity, called private
capital, which stood between mankind and the
possibility of pleasurable work.   This unusual road
which brought him to Socialism gave the peculiar

note to Morris's message.   One might have listened
to all the other great leaders—except, perhaps,
Bernard Shaw—and have thought that the collective system was the best kind of social structure
because it would reduce the hours of labour, pre-
vent waste, and divide the resulting wealth in a
fair proportion.   It was an ideal which might have
seemed compatible with a barrack-shaped factory,
and a well-drilled army of workers, pulling or push-
ing knobs which controlled an inferno of noisy
machinery;   the whole erection worked on the
principle of getting the job done as cheaply as
possible, and so that it could finish at the earliest
possible hour.   In other words, one might imagine
that the daily work is something to get through
quickly in order that the pleasure of leisure may
begin.   Morris tore this shallow doctrine to shreds
and, speaking with the weighty experience of more
mastered trades than any one else had to his credit
(for he was poet, painter, weaver, dyer, printer,
illuminator, romancer, all in one), he said that in
happy labour alone could a healthy normal human
being find joy.   Life was not in holidays, but in work
days.

It is obvious that this outlook must, if accepted,
profoundly concern the Socialist problem of the
organization of labour.   If the manufacture of
goods is to be no longer guided merely by the laws
of the cheapest supply and the quickest production,
but rather by a standard which will give happiness to the manufacturer, then the organization of work under Socialism will be infinitely

H

more than a change from private to collective control. It will be a change from production for the satisfaction of the market to production for the satisfaction of the worker's individual sense of creative fitness. The factory system may be the best way of multiplying goods at the fastest rate, just as it is easier to work to a set pattern instead of attempting to suit each personal fancy. But immediately one conceives, as Morris did, of the community as a group of craftsmen whose whole essence of life is the enjoyment of their labour and their individual creative skill, then the factory, with its standards of material economy, may—indeed, must—be put on one side as a ridiculous waste of good time. Again, if it is discovered that the continual doing of one kind of special work is displeasing to the cultured mind, then the specialization of labour must be given up, even though it interferes with the laws of economy. Again, the worker must be pampered by giving him the opportunity to change his place of work; says Morris: "A due amount of easily conceivable arrangement would enable me to make shoes in Rome, say, for three months, and to come back with new ideas of building, gathered from the sight of the work of past ages, amongst other things, which would perhaps be of service in London." When that sentence is carefully analysed it will be seen to approach the great subject of the organization of labour with very different objects than the production of the cheapest articles. Its first care is the welfare of that most delicate of all

machinery, the human mind ; all else gives way
to its welfare. But Morris was no unbalanced
fanatic ; he did not wildly crusade against all
machinery, as do some of his pseudo-disciples to-
day. It had its legitimate place on all occasions
where it did work which was necessary, but still
somewhat uninteresting ; it was entirely a matter
of detail, to be judged by the desire of the intelligent
worker, who would not use it if he could get more
pleasure from his work without it.

Such is Morris's unique contribution to Socialist
thought : the conception of the community labouring as much for pleasure in the work itself as for
the gain in wages or leisure after it is done. But
his directly political attitude is also of unusual
interest. The following words express the bond
between his art and his politics : " Popular art has
no chance of a healthy life, or, indeed, of a life at
all, till we are on the way to fill up the terrible gulf
between riches and poverty. Doubtless many
things will go in filling it up, and if art must be
one of these things, let it go. What business have
we with art at all unless all can share it ? . . .
For, after all, what is the true end and aims of all
politics and all commerce ? Is it not to bring about
a state of things in which all men may live at peace
and free from overburdensome anxiety, provided
with work which is pleasant to them and producing results useful to their neighbours ? " These
are the words of the man who loved art as much as
any man could love it, unreservedly admitting that
if he had to choose between the abolition of poverty

and the preservation of art, then he would declare
for the former.   If he were offered his little coterie
of cultured ease living on the degradation of
the multitude, then he would fling it back with
scorn.   As a matter of fact, Morris thought of
reform as needful almost as much for the rich as
the poor.   He wanted to destroy the slums, but
he wanted to destroy gentility also : " I have been
sickened by the stupidity of the mean idiotic rabbit
warrens that rich men build for themselves in Bays-
water and elsewhere : a vulgar stuccoed house
crowded with upholstery that I despise, in all re-
spects degrading to the mind and enervating to the
body."   It is not surprising that a man who thought
in this manner did not fit conveniently into the
ordinary political groove.   Cheap dwellings for the
working class seemed a strange ideal to one who
was out to get fine dwellings for all.   He did not feel
much inclined to discuss how London could be
made sanitary ; what the London County Council
could do or not do : he dismissed London altogether as
a hideous nightmare, a wholly monstrous evil.   The
City he roundly calls a " swindling ken " ; the
Council is a " barbarous half-hatched body of fools "
(this of the Council which the Fabian Society is
diligently labouring to reform).   In short, all that
Morris considered as Reform was outside the
possible scope of parliamentary action in his time.
Mere political reform he laughed at : he asks his
audience to consider the example of America—" a
country with universal suffrage, no king, no House
of Lords, no privilege as you fondly think ; only

a little standing army, chiefly used for the murder of red-skins ; a democracy after your model ; and with all that a society corrupt to the core, and at this moment engaged in suppressing freedom with just the same reckless brutality and blind ignorance as the Czar of all the Russias uses." Co-operation he thought equally futile : " The enormous commercial success of the great co-coperative societies, and the absolute no-effect of that success on the social conditions of the workers, are sufficient tokens of what this non-political co-operation must come to : nothing—it shall not be less." Even Socialist measures, such as the nationalization of land and railways, would not by themselves make any real change in the present system. In the total result, participation in the present parliamentary system meant continual compromising of Socialist principles, and very little, if any, result for the pains. So Morris laid it down that political action was waste of time, that for the present the business of Socialists was to educate the public mind. So he would have nothing to do either with the Social Democrats, who preached political independence, or with the Fabians, who allowed themselves to be made the cat's-paw of the Whigs. He admitted that this dread of political life was largely a personal failing ; and by 1888 we find him admitting even that the transition period must be worked for and accepted as an instalment. But he himself stood beyond : the refuser of compromise ; the persistent prophet of Socialism and nothing short of it ; the scorner of tactics and diplomacy : " I am tired of

being mealy-mouthed," he said.   He went beyond
Mr. Hyndman in rigid independence ;   he went
beyond every one in his grasp of the truth that
Socialism is much more than a system of State
machinery.   It is a method of setting the individual
free to order his life as his possibility for happiness
best allows.

XIV

ROBERT BLATCHFORD

Born 1851. Apprenticed to trade at fourteen. In army from
1871 to 1877, retiring as sergeant. Then found he could
write, and wrote for *Sunday Chronicle* when it started in
1885. In 1891 founded *Clarion*, sacrificing a large salary
to do so. Was parliamentary candidate for Bradford in
1891, but discovered that active politics not his work, and
has devoted himself to propagandist journalism. Chief
books : *Merrie England, Britain for the British, God and My
Neighbour, Not Guilty*, etc.

WE have tried to weigh the merits and the
faults of the twelve men who have perhaps
the best right to be called the leaders of Socialism.
But you cannot have an army of leaders ; there
must be some one to follow behind. It occurred
to one clear-headed man, who thought in short
paragraphs, that it was time somebody set to work
to create an army to go after the great men who
were on in front. That man was Robert Blatchford,
who can manufacture Socialists more quickly than
any one else. Tipton Limited sells more packets of
tea than any other firm, Bever sells more soap ;
one factory makes most boots ; another most
chairs. Mr. Blatchford and *The Clarion* make more
Socialists than any rival establishment. When you
come to think it over carefully, this business of

making Socialists is the only real work to be done. Whilst those brilliant leaders are waving their swords and doing the heroic generally, Mr. Blatchford attends to business and makes converts. When every one is a Socialist, that is, when every one is intelligent, there will be no need for leaders. It is only sheep who need shepherds and dogs to herd them properly. Intelligent people will do what is right out of sheer intelligence. (There is really much saving of trouble by being intelligent.)

Mr. Blatchford's great qualification for the post of missionary-in-chief is the fact that he can say in one sentence what the gentlemen who write for *The Times* and other classical works take half a column to put down. If the best literary style is the style that is clearest, beyond all possibility of misunderstanding its meaning (which is not a bad test for people who set out to say something), then Mr. Blatchford writes better English than any other master except Shakespeare and the author of the Bab Ballads. Whether you agree with him or not, you certainly cannot misunderstand him. He is the only man who would make a suitable editor for the Book of Life, wherein, we are given to understand, everything will be put down with perfect precision and with intolerable clearness. One meditates on the editor of *The Clarion* sitting within the Golden Gate, writing up the biography of Jay Gould or the Duke of Slumdom, or Messrs. X, sweaters ; probably the brief paragraphs on ordinary professional men and manufacturers and tradesmen will not read more soothingly ; or on the

wage-earner who voted against the Labour candidate.
Their doings will be put down so that there cannot be
the slightest mistake. There will be nothing unkind ; it will only be clear truth. Mr. Blatchford
is never unkind to an opponent. Why should he
be unkind ? When he can merely tell the truth
about him. If I were a Liberal or a Tory politician
I would pray that Robert Blatchford might lose
his matchless skill of telling the plain truth (so
that it stands out like gold in the sun), and that
he would take to writing fierce invective and flowing
periods.

Mr. Blatchford wrote two books, one named
Merrie England and the other *Britain for the British.*
When he had finished them it was no longer possible
to plead that you could not understand what
Socialism is ; for these books tell you so precisely
and clearly that there is no possibility of misunderstanding. Further, they are so convincing that
every one who reads them becomes a Socialist—except the mentally deficient. There are about a
million people in England who would vote for a
Socialist candidate at the next election. There are
perhaps five million more who have read Mr. Blatchford's writings and are not convinced. This fact
confirms the statistical summary of Thomas Carlyle,
who estimated the population of the British Isles
as " thirty millions, mostly fools." This is how
Mr. Blatchford states his aim : " If I can make
my meaning plain to members of Parliament,
bishops, editors, and other half-educated persons,
and to labouring men and women who have had

but little schooling, and have never been used to think or care about Socialism, or economics, or politics, or ' any such dry rot '—as they would call them—if I can catch the ear of the heedless and the untaught, the rest of you cannot fail to follow." These two books are a kind of test of sanity ; if you cannot understand them, if you are not convinced by them, then you are ripe for a lunatic asylum, where they will let you out to vote Liberal or Tory at the next election, just for the sake of freedom of conscience ; though, as a matter of fact, there is no real reason why we should let out lunatics to vote Mr. Asquith or Mr. Balfour into power, when we do not let them out to murder and destroy. Liberal and Tory rule destroys lives by the million, whereas the most successful of homicidal lunatics never gets beyond his half-dozen successes. But to return to Mr. Blatchford ; this is how he states the case against mine owners. " Suppose you go to the Duke of Hebden Bridge and ask for an engagement as clerk at his Grace's colliery at a salary of £5000 a year. . . . Should I be offended with the Duke for refusing to pay me more than I am worth ? Should I accuse him of class hatred ? Not at all. Why should I be blamed for suggesting that it is folly to pay a duke more than he is worth ? Or why should the Duke mutter about class hatred if I suggest that we can get a colliery director at a lower salary than his Grace ? Talk about sentimentality ! Are we to pay a guinea each for dukes if we can get them three a penny ? It is not business." It would take *The Spectator* six columns to smash mining royalties like that; and then some one would declare that he was not convinced. Mr. Blatchford would convince the Duke himself—but then he only reads *The Times*, unfortunately.

Just think how mad must be the gentlemen who own castles and lands and factories and cities, and all those sort of things, that they ever allowed Robert Blatchford to start writing about Socialism. Why, if they had only had their wits about them they would have kept him in the Army, have made him a field-marshal, given him a kingdom, done anything which would have stopped that pen of his putting down its clear-cut thoughts. If I ran the Liberal Party I would offer the editor of *The Clarion* a peerage and £100,000 a year if he would spend his time in fishing or playing marbles, instead of writing. I would not undertake the negotiations myself, because I do not like being thrown out of the window. It would be a dangerous job to try to stop Robert Blatchford's pen. The ordinary bribes would seem so amusing to him. " Imagine," he writes, " either of your old comrades riding in a gingerbread coach to be bored at a prince's levee ! Presentation at Court ! Why, I have smoked a pipe with William Morris ! . . . Oh, you Emperor, there, in the cocked hat or the jackboots, would you be graciously pleased to stand out of our sunlight ? " It is very well that he cannot be bought over ; for it seems certain that he could make it perfectly clear, absolutely transparent, that the Liberals are really reformers after all. I do not believe there is any subject under the sun which Mr. Blatchford could not clearly explain in two paragraphs. Think of the headaches that would have been saved if he had written " Capital " instead of Marx ; or if he had written the first chapter of Mr. Meredith's *The Egoist,* or Robert Browning's *James Lee's Wife.* A sketch of Nietzsche's philosophy by Robert Blatchford would be invaluable. He might even give a reasonable explanation of the advantage the Fabian Society gets from supporting Liberal candidates. He could explain the Universe, for elementary schools, in a chapter of ordinary length. He spends his time explaining Socialism because it is the only subject which stands his searchlight ; it is the only philosophy and art of life which will stand the truth being told about it. It is Robert Blatchford's business to tell the clear truth about things. Socialism is the only subject which does not look stupid when he has finished with it. That is why he writes about Socialism.

That clear brain knows exactly what it wants. Mr. Blatchford wants a Socialist Party in Parliament and in every Town Council. He is quite clear as to his end, and quite clear about the manner of getting there. He says : " If 4,000,000 workers paid one penny a week (the price of a Sunday paper, or of a glass of cheap beer) they would have £866,000 at the end of a year. Election expenses of 200 Labour candidates at £500 each would be £100,000. Pay of Labour members at £200 a year would be £40,000. Total £140,000 : leaving a balance in hand of £726,000." Then 2,000 local councillors

and three Socialist newspapers and still a balance
of £476,000. But the four million workers are stupid
and don't pay that penny a week. It is Mr. Blatchford's business to make them wise. There is a ring
of fierce passionate anger against the injustice and
folly of the world beneath his calm sentences, a
satire which whips and flays. Unanswerable logic,
passionate earnestness, scorching sarcasm, these
are his ingredients ; and he mixes the three with
every paragraph he writes. Listen : " If I were a
docker, and if my wife had to go out in leaky boots,
or if my delicate child could not get sea air and
nourishing food, I should be apt to ask whether his
lordship, the great ground landlord, could not do
with less rent and his sweet wife with fewer pearls.
I should ask that. I should not think myself a
man if I did not ask it ; nor should I feel happy if
I did not strain every nerve to get an answer."